THE PROS

THE

PROS

By ROBERT LISTON

Illustrated by Jo Polseno

PLATT & MUNK, *Publishers* | NEW YORK

Acknowledgments

I've tried to name in the text all those publicity directors and other club officials who were so helpful to me. In addition I'd like to thank Leonard Koppett, John Steadman, Seth Goltzer, Mr. and Mrs. Richard Mariner, my wife Jean and, most especially, my editor Bernard Garfinkel, who played such an intimate role in planning this book and so often bolstered my frequently waning courage.

Library of Congress Catalog Card Number: 68–19582

To My Favorite Tennis Partner

Contents

The Pro

Bob Liston weighs in at 160 pounds and probably should be described as "a counter-puncher who always lasts the route." As writers go, he has deceptive moves. He reminds me of Cazzie Russell's story about his high school coach. The coach would have the team deliberately miss their shots in the first part of the warm-up period. Then, after the opposing team had finished their warm-up, the coach would order Russell and his teammates to pour baskets through the hoop, "psyching" the opponents out of their sneakers. Liston is like that.

We were having lunch at Le Marmiton, an eatery in New York that shelters writers and editors from book reviewers during the midday hours, and I suggested to him that a good idea for a book might be the one you are about to read. Liston made his dark eyes go wide behind his glasses. "It might be," he growled, "but it would take a whale of a lot of time and probably need someone with a lot of contacts. I don't think I could handle it, considering the kind of schedule I'm boxed into." Having come up against his deadpan style in the past, I pressed him, and by the time we had gotten through the *café filtre,* he had moved about three inches from his original judgment and was ready to dig around a little bit.

Three weeks later I got a note from him outlining the contents, suggesting various themes the book might explore, and rattling off a list of athletes who might be prospects for inclusion. He had decided, after all, that he could probably squeeze the project in. Six months later, the manuscript arrived in my office.

Like the athletes he got to see, Liston is "task-oriented," and once he steps up to the plate, he takes his cuts no matter what. My conception of the room in which he writes (I've never seen it) is that it has five or six typewriters lined up on a shelf and that on any given day his schedule is set up so that he can scurry from one typewriter to another, batting out chapters with the nifty ease of Billy Rose winning a shorthand contest or Mantle in his prime flashing down to first on a drag bunt. This is rather disconcerting to someone who often gets knotted up at the sight of a blank page in his typewriter.

The point of all this, aside from letting a little light fall on what has been a very pleasant relationship between an editor and a writer, is that Liston is a pro. And as a pro, he's turned in an enlightening report on the personalities, experiences and psyches of some men who are known to every sports fan in the country. More particularly, he's gone beyond the normal newspaper sports page gloss of what athletes are really like and set down some strong, straight and fascinating words that will, I hope, please everyone who reads this book. It's not easy to make any man reveal himself, and most men resist the attempt, but under Liston's level gaze, the men in this book talk about themselves honestly and directly. Obviously they found Bob Liston's moves just as deceptive as his editor does.

BERNARD GARFINKEL

THE PROS

The Line-Up

ONE of the marvels of our time is the popularity of professional athletics. Last year 25 million Americans attended major league baseball games and another 7,700,-000 sat in often-inclement weather to watch two professional football teams clash on Sunday afternoons. Millions more purchased tickets to see professional basketball, ice hockey, golf (standing all the while), tennis, soccer and other sports events. But those who actually attended the games were a minority. Tens of millions more watched on television or listened to the radio.

Professional athletics are the spectacles of our era. They can be compared to the Greek Olympic games, to the contests of Roman gladiators, to medieval jousting tournaments, and they are flavored with the same pomp and ceremony that characterized European monarchies in their heyday.

Professional athletics are also big business. Teams are bought and sold for millions of dollars – although their assets often do not include buildings or real estate. All that is sold are the players, a handful of administrative personnel — and the potential for profit. The teams themselves make a great deal of money from the sale of tickets, radio and television rights, programs, souvenirs and concessions. And many other often distantly related businesses stand to profit. Sporting goods firms sell their products to young people and amateur athletes. Radio and television networks receive tens of millions of dollars in revenue from sponsors of games, and, in turn, the commercial sponsors sell products that are identified with professional sports and the men who play them. Restaurateurs, cab drivers, street vendors and many other small businessmen are enriched during the holiday atmosphere that accompanies the games. Surely the abolishment of professional sports would create an economic slump.

Some of the highest rewards our society can offer are lavished upon professional athletes. The most successful and popular are paid salaries of $100,000 a year and more. These earnings are further enlarged by fees from personal appearances, product endorsements and related business activities, making top players millionaires. Indeed, golfers Arnold Palmer and Jack Nicklaus are said to earn one million dollars a year from a combination of prize money and business interests.

The professional athlete has replaced the movie star as our leading celebrity. He becomes a movie and television star, like Chuck Conners, Ron Ely and Jim Brown. He is interviewed and his opinions sought on such subjects as civil rights, religion and foreign policy. His character is cited as an example to be emulated by children. He is made a director of large corporations, elected to public office, named to the Supreme Court of the United States and selected by the President to head a nationwide physical fitness program. He writes books and tens of thousands of people buy them. Routinely he becomes a sportscaster or commentator. He makes guest appearances on television shows. His name becomes a household word, his face is known to millions, and in his old age he is remembered and respected. His passing is marked by a long obituary in the newspaper and perhaps a public monument. Because of all this, fathers encourage their sons to throw a football or baseball, for to excel in professional athletics is a high road to fame and wealth.

This book is about professional athletes. It is, in simplest terms, a report of interviews with 12 professional athletes and with a non-playing professional football man. The players are a diverse group. Some are superstars at the peak of their careers. Others are little known to the public. They range in experience from a hopeful rookie to a retired player no longer active in his sport.

The idea behind the interviews was to discover what kind of men become professional athletes, to explore their aspirations, motivations, problems, rewards. I hoped to learn why one man succeeds brilliantly and another fails; what professional sports demand from a man in return for wealth and fame; whether there is a similarity between, say, a football, baseball or basketball player and a golfer. I had many questions. Are size and physical ability all that matter? Or are there other factors which create success? Do the pros deserve the public's high esteem? Are the qualities which bring success in sports worthy of admiration by a young man who wants to be a doctor, lawyer, artist or bricklayer?

I chose the men I did because they seemed likely to provide answers to these questions. Among those I interviewed are men with great natural ability and others with only limited talent. There are some who achieved instant stardom, others who never made it, still others who had it taken away from them. Some are the sons of athletes who grew up with a compulsion to be a pro, others never had the remotest idea of playing.

I wanted players who would have a wide appeal, whose background and accomplishments would be interesting and who would be articulate about telling their story. I wanted to talk to a college star on the eve of turning pro to discover his hopes and motivations. I wanted to interview a college star the year after he turned pro to discover how – and why – his hopes had materialized. I hoped to get one player of limited physical talent who became a star. How did he do it? And then I wanted a player of great physical ability who flopped so I could ask him why. I wanted to see a retired superstar whose records had been broken, a player who had had stardom taken away from him by injury, an "average player" who was neither famous nor wealthy, so that I could ask him what he achieved from his labors. And I wanted to talk to an owner, general manager and manager about their jobs.

There is a common background to all the interviews which ought to be explained. I began each interview by saying, "I'm not a sportswriter." The athletes had various reactions to the phrase. Some simply nodded in acceptance. Others smiled sympathetically. A few uttered a hearty and approving, "Good!"

Next I asked indulgence for my lack of expertise. I usually said something like this: "Because I am not a sportswriter, I may ask you some stupid or embarrassing questions. If I do, it's unintentional. Just straighten me out."

This speech, entirely honest and not the least ingenuous, was effective. During the interviews the pros were exceedingly patient with me. They took time to explain the ABC's of their craft to this unabashed tyro and were generally helpful in many ways.

I suspect almost any 12-year-old boy can recite batting averages with more authority than I can. I'm quite sure most readers can give a better explanation of a football trap play. Actually, I've been a militant non-athlete all my life. In high school, I held the strikeout record. At bat seven times, struck out seven times. I never even hit a foul ball. I learned to swim as an adult, but only to the point where I can thrash along for about 15 feet — as long as the water isn't over my head. The only sport in which I have any proficiency, and that is not a great deal, is tennis.

A man does not, of course, have to be an athlete to be a sportswriter. But a sportswriter is a specialist. He has a thorough knowledge of at least one sport. He knows the terminology, techniques, strategy. He has encyclopedic knowledge of past events, performances and performers in this sport. He is or should be an excellent critic of a current performance. And, of course, the best of them are excellent writers. Sportswriting is colorful, full of marvelous words and phrases such as "wallop," "crunching," "rhubarb," "swivel hip," "looper," "dunk," "gridiron" and hundreds more which writers on more prosaic subjects can only envy. The best sportswriters frequently cross over into non-sportswriting with great success. Names such as Gallico, Lardner, Considine, Linn, Breslin come to mind. But I am hard-pressed to think of a single non-sportswriter who successfully invaded the sports field, with the possible exception of George Plimpton who wrote *Paper Lion* and *Out of My League*, after getting on the field with the Detroit Lions and the New York Yankees.

I haven't tried to be a sportswriter in the traditional sense. I did not ask Billy Casper what grip he uses (although he told me), or Johnny Unitas how he throws the forward pass (but the subject did come up) or Bob Feller how he threw the curve ball (yet he did give an impromptu demonstration). I simply attempted to discover what I could about professional athletes — *as men.*

I feel that I succeeded. I found each man to be unique. Some were gentle and soft spoken, others were terse and blunt. Religion was a major factor in the lives of a few, not at all in others. Natural leadership was an outstanding quality in some, others were content to follow another man. Each man was different in personality, background, experience and attitudes, yet there were similarities among all. What they had in common was a great love for the sport they play, dedication, willingness to work long and hard to perfect their abilities. The motivation of the most successful was not to achieve wealth and fame, though none objected to that, but rather to excel in an activity that is extraordinarily demanding of them physically, mentally and psychologically. To succeed, they must do what few ordinary men can do, coordinate the body, the mind and the emotions to achieve a peak performance – and do it, not just occasionally, but consistently.

It is a temptation to take these and other similarities and draw broad conclusions about *all* professional athletes and the ingredients of their success or failure. I will resist the temptation, for 13 men cannot, of course, be definitive. I'm sure there are pros who hate their sport, do not work hard and have motives less admirable than the men interviewed for this book.

I didn't investigate all types of pros. There are no boxers, tennis pros, soccer players or billiards champs in this book. I restricted myself to the sports which, I felt, aroused the fan's greatest admiration and interest – football, baseball, basketball, hockey and golf. Boxing fans may dispute this, and with good reason perhaps, but sport has always had its disagreements. Horseracing might well qualify, but it seems to me that the horse gets much of the credit. I did interview a horse years ago, but only the horse and I took it seriously.

What could be a problem in a book like this is that some time elapses between the interview and publication. But I think this is an advantage. When a player speaks of his hopes and determinations for the season just ahead (either the 1967 or 1968 season), the reader will know how things turned out. The player may have been released, traded, broken a leg, been arrested for speeding – or achieved greater success than he hoped for. But the reader will know how the athlete felt on a given day or two in the past, and he will know what the player did not know – how the future would turn out.

I chose the men in this book with the help of a newspaper sportswriter, and with the advice of several knowledgeable friends. Some candidates were uninterested, unavailable or simply did not reply to letters. But, after many frustrations, and some substitutions, I succeeded in arranging the interviews. Readers may quarrel with the selections and be disappointed that their favorite is omitted, but I hope all will agree with me that the men they are about to meet are interesting fellows.

RAYMOND BERRY

82
82
JP

Raymond Berry

"My whole life and ambition could be summarized in just one sentence: I just had to play football."

THE BALTIMORE COLTS train on the campus of Westminster College in Westminster, Maryland, a small town about 30 miles northwest of Baltimore. The college is situated on a hilltop at the northern edge of town, and the campus is pleasant, with lovely tree-shaded walks that circle a cluster of neo-Colonial buildings. I knew that professional football teams often trained at small colleges in small towns. I wondered why, then reflected that a small college would provide the necessary facilities — gridiron and dormitories — yet keep the team sheltered from distractions. The empty Westminster campus certainly seemed to be an atmosphere conducive to hard work and study.

Except for the lack of posters, pennant and the usual undergraduate paraphernalia, Raymond Berry's room might have belonged to a college freshman. It was on the second floor of a long dormitory, one of three rooms with a common doorway. In the center was a young player, whom I never did meet but who seemed to be studying incessantly.

I arrived about 9:30 in the evening. At that advanced stage of training, the Colts had scheduled for the next day a morning meeting, an afternoon practice and a two-hour club meeting in the evening. Berry and I would have an hour or so to talk before he went to bed.

I had come to see Berry because I wanted to talk to a player with limited physical ability who had become a star. I thought immediately of Berry, the great split end of the Colts. I had been a newspaper reporter in Baltimore for several years. Anyone living in Baltimore cannot help but be exposed to the adored Colts; from July to January, the sports pages of the Baltimore papers are filled with information about the team and its players.

Next to Johnny Unitas, the player most written about is Raymond Berry. There are always stories about his lack of speed, average size and poor eyesight. At least once a season newspapers carry a photograph of the whole team down on all fours scouring the turf for one of Berry's lost contact lenses. Yet, somehow, he had made himself into the greatest end in the history of professional football. That accolade rests upon the fact he has caught more passes for more yardage than anyone who ever played the game.

Berry seemed the logical choice for this category, yet a number of people discouraged me from selecting him. The sportswriter I spoke to said, "Yes, Berry would be good, but I think Maury Wills would be better. He's the greatest base stealer who ever played baseball, yet he's not particularly fast, not particularly anything. He did it by hard work and application." Shortly thereafter, a Baltimore sportswriter said, "Berry's not a good interview. You won't get much of a story there."

So I decided to seek an interview with Maury Wills. After his great years with the Los Angeles Dodgers, Wills had been traded before the 1967 season to the Pittsburgh Pirates. Since, at that time, I hoped to interview Harry Walker, the Pirates manager, it made sense to try for both men. I made phone calls to Pittsburgh and wrote letters.

At the same time I was trying to arrange an interview with Johnny Unitas. Harry Hulmes, the Colts' general manager, and Jim Walker, the publicity director, were not encouraging. After talking to Unitas, they reported that he was cool to the idea. Hulmes said, "Everybody wants to interview Unitas. You'd think we had no other players on the team. Raymond Berry, for example, has a great story."

Shortly thereafter, Harry Walker was fired as the Pittsburgh manager and Maury Wills said no to my request, so I abandoned my plans to go to Pittsburgh. All of a sudden Berry again seemed to be the logical choice. And he might provide an entree to Unitas. I knew Berry and Unitas were friends. If I went to the Colts training camp to interview Berry, I might get to see Unitas, too.

Asked by Walker, Berry readily agreed to the interview, but requested that it be delayed a month, until after August 15. As Walker explained it, "There will be two-a-day practices until then. No one works harder than Raymond. He's just worn out at the end of the day."

Now, a month later, I stepped into Berry's room. He was sprawled backwards, that is feet at the head, on the lower of two steel bunks. The room was neat, but gave the impression that he was only a temporary resident. The open closet contained a small collection of sports shirts, slacks and a jacket, two pairs of brown shoes (size 12 at least) and a suitcase into which all this could be crammed at a moment's notice. There were two desks. One displayed the Colts' black leather-covered looseleaf playbook. The other desk was cluttered with a significant pile of fan mail. There were several books in the room: *Applied Bible; Bible Handbook;* Billy Graham's *World Aflame; Ben Hur; Rise and Fall of the Third Reich; Courage to Conquer.* Berry stood up, shook hands, motioned to a seat, then resumed his former position.

Raymond Berry is 34, so it would be an exaggeration to say he looks like a college freshman, but finding him in a college dormitory did not seem the least surprising. He has an unlined boyish face with a grin of pure innocence, clear blue eyes and neat, short-cropped brown hair. Brown-rimmed glasses add to the impression of studiousness. His physique in no way resembles that to be expected in a football player. He is tall and lithe. No ripple of muscles bulges under his tee shirt and brown slacks. He appears to be in flawless physical condition, but he might be a salesman or teacher who keeps in shape. He talks quietly and slowly in a Texas drawl, weighing his words, and seems to enjoy being interviewed. I got the overwhelming impression that he is a shy and gentle man.

I told him I always associated him with the finest compliment I'd ever heard about a football player. Some years ago, after a particularly good game, the Baltimore papers had quoted a defensive back as saying Berry was unbelievable. The back claimed to know precisely what Berry was going to do, every fake, every step, yet Berry did exactly what was expected and caught the pass anyhow. Berry had not read the comment and was amused. "And here I thought I was fooling them all this time."

Berry had a somewhat different view of his physical limitations than sportswriters or fans. He was six-feet-two, 185 pounds. "This is about average for offensive ends," he said. "The public has the impression ends are bigger than they are." His eyesight is definitely not average. "I'm very nearsighted. I can't see a single letter on the eyechart, not even the big E. But my vision is fully correctable, so I don't consider it a handicap."

I asked about speed. "I don't have great speed," he said. "I'll do 40 yards in four minutes, nine seconds. Most other ends and defensive backs will run it in 4.6 or 4.7. But I don't think it makes that much difference. I've never felt overwhelmed by anyone's speed. When going for the ball, lack of speed is no disadvantage."

Despite Berry's tendency to play down his physical limitations, the fact was that he brought neither outstanding size nor speed to the game. (I discovered later that huge linemen can run the 40 in 4.9) I asked him how he had been able to catch more passes than anyone else in the history of football.

His instant reply: "There is no doubt in my mind how to account for it. The Lord. He's the source of all my athletic ability." In saying this, Berry was not speaking lightly. He is, as I discovered in talking to him, a deeply religious man who believes his life is guided by God's will.

I asked him what ability compensated for his physical limitations?

"My hands," he said. "If I get to a football I can catch it. I've been able to catch a football since I was a kid. It's a gift. I can catch a lot of balls that seem like they can't be caught."

His words brought forth a mental image of innumerable Berry circus catches. Berry going high in the air with two defenders and coming down with the football. Berry leaping over the sideline marker, clutching the ball with his fingertips and falling, his feet inbounds. Berry reaching behind him, while running at full speed, to pull in a pass that was thrown short. Berry diving to snare a pass everyone thought wide of its mark.

"The Lord gave me the ability to catch the football. But it is up to me to make the most of it. I've always felt it was the worst thing in the world to drop a football. If the pass gets to me, I'm supposed to catch it. If I drop it, I'm letting down the Lord, my teammates, myself. I'm not earning my salary."

I asked how many he dropped a season. "Two, maybe three," he said.

"Catching the football is a matter of practice. I get as much pass catching drill as I can. I catch maybe 30 or 40 balls a day. If we're running plays in practice, I'll get somebody to throw me a ball or two on the way back to the huddle. If the team is working on running plays, I'll catch a couple of balls during that time. If I drop a ball, I try to figure out why. I didn't turn my body right. My hands weren't in the right position. I did something wrong or I would have caught it. So I get somebody to throw me that pass over and over until I correct my mistake."

I've interviewed many men who have said they take their strengths for granted, while working to improve their weaknesses. Berry did the opposite. He had, as he said, the innate ability to catch a football. He considered it God's gift. He practiced running pass patterns, faking, blocking and other skills, but his major effort went into improving his pass catching, which had always been his greatest talent.

"The forward pass is the product of an immense amount of practice," he said. "Say I'm running a deep pass pattern. I come off the line, go into my fake to pull the defender out of position and break downfield. I try to go as fast as I can, for I have to assume the quarterback is going to overthrow the ball, not underthrow. I don't know exactly what the quarterback does — you'll have to ask John [Unitas] about that — but he releases the ball about the time I make my break, throwing to a spot somewhere downfield. Now, he has specified the approximate area in the huddle, but the exact spot will be determined by a number of factors, including the position of the defenders, the amount of time he has to get the pass off, and, of course, my speed. By the time I've made three or four strides after the break, I have to look back and spot the ball and never take my eye off it. If the play is correctly executed, I should run right under the ball.

"But the timing must be precise. Back when I first made my break, John had to calculate within a matter of inches how much ground I'd cover at top speed and how high I'd be able to leap. This can be done only with incessant practice, so that John knows exactly the point I'm capable of reaching, and I know where he'll throw in relation to the defenders and whether it will be a soft pass, hard pass, high trajectory or low.

"A receiver hopes to have enough practice with a quarterback to perfect this timing and coordination. After all, a quarterback can only throw so many balls during a practice and there are many receivers. That's why it is hard for the back-up quarterback to break into the lineup. He simply hasn't had enough practice with the number one receivers. The same is true with the substitute receivers going into the game with the number one quarterback. Under our system, if the second quarterback has to go into the game, the reserve receivers usually go in, too. They've had more practice together."

Berry was talking easily, warming up to the subject.

"From experience I know there are certain situations that are going to come up frequently, so I try to get as much work on them as I can. For example, on a short pass, I know I'm going to have to go up in the air and fight the defender for the ball. The natural instinct is to think about the defender rather than the ball. I've trained myself to keep my eye on the ball and think only about catching it and not concern myself with the defender. I practice this. I get somebody to throw the ball and a defender to work with me. We practice together, going up in the air and fighting for the ball until, in a game I know instinctively how to catch and hold on to the ball.

"Another game situation. You're breaking down the field and you look over your right shoulder for the pass. But because of the position of a defender, the pass is coming over your left shoulder. Without losing stride, you have to turn and look the other way. This means taking your eye off the ball. You have to practice making that turn and spotting the ball quickly.

"Or say it's a sideline or end zone pass. The rule says the receiver must have both feet inbounds when he catches the ball. This is hard to do, but if you practice enough, you can learn to leap in the air, catch the ball out of bounds, stick your feet as far back of you as you can and then relax, so you fall like a rock. Everything may be out of bounds but your feet, but it's a legal reception. It takes drill to train yourself to do this."

If one single play is associated with Raymond Berry, it is the sideline pass. He has caught so many of them that Baltimore sportswriters consider the Unitas to Berry sideline pass the Colts' substitute for the end sweep. Berry makes a quick fake, breaks for the sideline and catches the ball with only his feet inbound. As executed by these two, this is a difficult play to defend.

Next to Berry's ability to catch the football, the most amazing aspect of his career has been his durability. He was starting his thirteenth season with the Colts. He had caught 620 passes in those years, but he had also endured a greater number of savage blocks and teeth-rattling tackles. It is a perfectly respectable play for the cornerback, safety or linebacker to pile into the receiver as hard as he can to knock the ball loose. Every fan has groaned when he's seen a 225-pound linebacker charge full speed into a 185-pound end at the precise moment he is stretched full length in a leap to receive a pass. I asked Berry if this didn't worry him.

"No, I've never been bothered particularly by contact in a game. I twisted my knee once on a bad piece of turf. Twice I was injured in collisions with my own men, but being tackled has never bothered me."

Berry's durability is also a product of practice. "The Lord gave me this body, but it is up to me to condition myself. I work out all winter and spring so that I stay in shape. I do weightlifting and I use apparatus to develop my muscles. In training, I work with the blocking sled to get my body used to accepting heavy blows. Then I run a lot to improve my wind. I have a regular conditioning program. I know just how hard to work so that I'm tired, but not overworked. When we start the season, I'm ready. I am right now. I suppose I should be feeling my age, but I don't. In fact, I ran faster in time trials this year than last."

It was eleven o'clock and Berry had a hard day ahead of him. I arranged to meet him the following morning and I left. But I didn't stop thinking about him. I felt I had obtained what I came for, some understanding of how a player of limited physical talents becomes a star in a physically demanding sport. He practices and drills to the point of near exhaustion. He gets himself in peerless physical shape – at an age when most men are going soft and enjoying that second helping of pie alamode – and he works to make the best use of his natural gifts. But if I had some understanding of what Berry had done, I had no idea *why* he had done it. What would drive a man to perfect techniques in a sport where he was something of a physical misfit? No one would have to ask why Wilt Chamberlain plays basketball. Sheer physical size would dictate it. Or why 300-pound Roger Brown is a defensive lineman for the Los Angeles Rams. But why would Berry want to work so hard when, physically, he did not seem at all suited for the game? I had to get an answer to that the next day.

When I saw Berry again, the scene was the same, except for the daylight in the room. Berry still wore a tee shirt and brown pants and still reclined on the bed. I asked him why he played football.

He hesitated, thinking about his answer. "I've thought a lot about that, believe me I have. There's no doubt in my mind that playing football just came naturally. There was nothing else for me to do. You see the Lord had a hand on my life long before I knew it or understood it."

I asked him how he got started.

"I was born and raised in Paris, Texas, which is about 100 miles northeast of Dallas. My father coached the high school football team, but I can't say he ever pressured me to play. It was just as natural as breathing. I had always liked rough play. A knockdown, dragout game of anything was for me. When I started to play organized football, I just naturally excelled at it. Nothing ever happened to discourage me. In the seventh and eighth grades, I was named to the all-city team. In high school I was first team in the district and second team in the state.

"By that time all I lived for was football. My whole life and ambition could be summarized in one sentence: I just had to play football in the Southwest Conference. Can you understand that? Do you have any idea what Southwest Conference football means to a Texas boy?"

I knew exactly what he meant. About the time he was in junior high school, I lived in Texas and became acquainted with the football fanaticism of Texans. A surefire argument resulted when any Texan discovered I was from Ohio and rooted for Ohio State. The Big Ten Conference, to which Ohio State belonged, was widely reported to play the best brand of college football in the country, a contention heatedly disputed by any loyal son of Texas. To him *real* football was played in the Southwest Conference. Any other brand of football was questionable. This attitude still exists today. Just listen as the television announcer reads off the home towns of Southwest Conference players. Almost to a man they are from Texas. Texas boys play football in Texas.

"But no Southwest Conference school offered me a scholarship. The coaches all knew I could catch the ball, but I weighed only 150 pounds, far too light to play their brand of football. I was determined to play in the conference. The only way I could figure to do it was to play junior college football for a year. If I excelled there, maybe a conference school would offer me a scholarship.

So I enrolled in Schreiner Junior College in Kerrville, Texas. I started out on the third team, but a week before the season opened, the two guys in front of me were both hurt. I started the first game and scored a touchdown. I went on to have a real good year, leading the junior college conference in receptions.

"I figured that would surely get me accepted in the Southwest Conference, but it didn't. All any of the coaches could see was that I weighed 165 pounds, which was still not enough. But I did get one expression of interest, and this forced the decision that changed my life. Rusty Russell, head coach at SMU was stressing the passing game at that time. He knew I could catch the football and he knew I was still growing, but he didn't have much faith I'd grow big enough. He was willing to put me on the red shirt team – the pros would call it the taxi squad – for a year. I'd work out against the variety, and he'd evaluate me. If I showed enough ability and grew big enough, he'd offer me a scholarship. If not, I'd have to go back to junior college. I thought about it and decided this was my only chance to play in the Southwest Conference, so I took it.

"I'll never forget that year. I was keyed up for every practice like it was a bowl game. I really went all out. And I was fortunate. SMU's quarterback was Fred Benners, the leading passer in the conference. The job of the red shirt team was to run the opponents' offensive plays against the defensive team. Benners did the passing and I did the catching and in every practice I caught passes all over the field. Coach Russell had no choice but to offer me a scholarship.

"The next year, my junior year, I played on the second team because I wasn't considered a good enough blocker. But I got to play about a third of the time and had a fair year. My senior year I made varsity. I was elected co-captain and named to a couple of All-American teams. But by this time SMU was stressing the running game, so I didn't catch too many passes. However, I did score two touchdowns against Notre Dame that year and one of about 60 yards which was nullified by a penalty."

I asked how he came to the Colts.

"You have to understand that until the last few years no one in Texas paid much attention to pro football. College ball in the Southwest Conference was all that mattered. But I'd started to watch a little pro football on television while at SMU, mainly because Doak Walker, a great favorite in Texas, was quarterback for the Detroit Lions. I began to get interested, and since I felt I could catch the football as well as anyone, I realized that if I got the chance to play with the pros, I'd take it.

"To my great surprise the Colts drafted me as a future at the end of my junior year. The choice was no great vote of confidence. I think the Colts picked me on the twentieth round, but the selection gave me a tremendous lift. It meant I'd have a chance to play pro ball after college.

"Being selected by the Colts was another great event in my life. I often wondered what would have happened if I'd been drafted by a team like the Rams or Browns. They already had great ends. I'm sure I would have sat on the bench or been released. But the Colts were a new team and building for the future. There were 14 rookies on a squad of 33 that year, including quarterback George Shaw, Alan Ameche at fullback, Dick Syzmanski at center, halfback L. G. Dupre and George Preas on the offensive line. Shaw of course got hurt a year later, which gave Unitas his big chance. But those fellows who started when I did formed the nucleus of our championship teams in '58 and '59."

Berry neglected to mention that he was a key member of those teams. His 12 receptions in the 1958 sudden death playoff game against the Giants is still an NFL record.

I asked him whom he replaced at split end, which struck me as a first class "trivia" question, on a par with asking who played first base for the Yankees after Lou Gehrig. I remember the day Babe Dahlgren substituted for the immortal Iron Man, but I could never have guessed Berry's predecessor. "A fellow by the name of Lloyd Colteryahn," Berry answered.

Berry had portrayed a young man with a virtual compulsion to play football who overcame his small stature, his average speed and his poor eyesight by the single-minded development of his asset, his ability to catch a football. I wanted to know what had fueled his great desire.

"In the beginning I guess it was a desire for personal glory. Football was my god. It was all I lived for. All I wanted in life was to be a big star in the Southwest Conference. I guess every Texas boy feels that way at one time or other in his life, but I never got over it and I was never going to be able to live with myself if I didn't try. I had to be the best there was in the best college conference. When I came with the Colts, it was the same. I just had to be the best pass receiver in this league.

"It is different now. Seven years ago I accepted Christ as my Savior. My purpose in life is to do what God wants me to do. Football is no longer my God. I live for only one Person and that is Christ."

I asked what led to his conversion.

"It was no sudden thing. I had become aware that I had no purpose in life, no direction. I lacked inner peace. I was rooming on the road with Don Shinnick, one of our linebackers. He had accepted Christ as his Savior some years before, and we talked about it from time to time. I started to read the Bible and soon couldn't get enough of it. I realized that I had a lot to thank God for and that my abilities were no accident. I still don't belong to any formal church, but I think of myself as a Christian."

I asked if he believed it was God's will for him to play football.

"I'm right where I'm supposed to be. If I didn't feel that way, I couldn't play the game. I'm not real sure what God's purpose is in having me play football, but I'm absolutely sure this is what I'm supposed to do. My task is to give my best effort to every part of my job. To do less than my best is a reflection on my Savior."

Berry admitted that before every game he experienced great personal anxiety. "I don't really understand it, but it's a great fear that I won't play well, that I'll miss a pattern or drop a pass, that I'll fail everyone, the Lord, my teammates, the fans, the owners who pay my salary.

I've an obligation to all these people. I've thought a lot about this anxiety, and as near as I can figure, I'm afraid my will won't prevail. This is wrong, of course. So I usually pray to God for forgiveness and tell Him I'm ready to accept His will. I feel better after that."

Berry has no regular off-season job. He lives in Lutherville, a Baltimore suburb, with his wife, a former Texas girl, and his young son and daughter. In the spring, he goes back to Texas and coaches pass receivers at Baylor University during spring practice. He does some work with the Billy Graham Organization, but he has made no plans for a career after his playing days are over. He says: "I'm sure the Lord will make His purpose known to me when He is ready."

Raymond Berry goes against the popular image of the professional football player as a brawny, two-fisted tough guy. He is shy, studious, gentle, introspective and, at least when I was with him, totally uncombative. Yet he enjoys the rough body contact of football, and in his enjoyment, he has caught more passes for more yardage than any end in NFL history. What Berry's career demonstrates is that desire and discipline are at least as important as talent. With Ray Berry as an example, every coach ought to look for players who have gentle dispositions, average size, average speed and poor eyesight — as long as they love the game.

JOHNNY UNITAS

19
JP

Johnny Unitas

"I've never been upset over anything more than five minutes in my life."

THERE IS, I believe, an image of Johnny Unitas which every sports fan will recall. Say the Colts are playing Green Bay in a game that will decide the conference title. It is late in the fourth quarter and the Packers are leading by a field goal. The Colts are on offense and driving. Unitas is clicking on short passes to Berry and John Mackey, his tight end. Then a pass fails and a trap play up the middle gains only a couple of yards. It is third and eight at midfield. The Colts huddle, line up and Unitas leans over the center. Seconds later he is going back to pass. It is a crucial third down play and probably any coach would be satisfied to have this quarterback running it. He drops back into the pocket, cocks his arm and pumps once toward the right, then turns to pass to the left, to Berry. At that instant he is smothered by the on-charging defensive end, Willie Davis. The play is broken, the game is lost and with the game go the Colts' title hopes.

Then comes the image. The television camera shows the teams running off the field. One man, Johnny Unitas, walks slowly to the sidelines. He is a picture of total dejection, head down, shoulders slumped, arms hanging loosely. His steps are slow and appear to be painful, like those of an old man climbing steep stairs. You cannot help feeling sorry for him: he is a man in deep anguish.

Now, go with me to a dormitory at Westminster College. I had come to see Ray Berry, hoping I'd get to Unitas, too. At the end of my first session with Berry, I asked him if he'd speak to John on my behalf. He agreed and next morning said Unitas would be glad to see me. After my interview with Berry, I stuck my head into John's room.

It should be remembered that a great deal of telephoning and letter writing had preceded my appearance. Two Colts officials and a sportswriter had supposedly been in touch with Unitas about me, not to mention Berry. Yet, when I introduced myself, I might have been a little green man from Mars. I told him Harry Hulmes and Jim Walker had spoken to him about me. He said, "Nobody ever said anything to me." They had, but he'd simply forgotten. I was flustered, and I'm sure I stammered. "What did you want?" he asked. I told him, in a rather stumbling way, about the book. He said, "Sure, I'll talk to you," and told me to come back at two o'clock that afternoon, since he had to attend a team meeting in the meanwhile.

Unitas and I walked out of the dormitory together. At the dormitory entrance we parted. I took a few steps, then looked back as Unitas walked across the lawn toward the adjoining building. He was the same picture of total dejection, head down, arms dangling. He had the same slump, the identical old man's step.

I found Unitas' walk intriguing because I wanted to ask him about the effect of aging on an athlete. I wanted to know what adjustments a quarterback makes as his reflexes slow, the spring goes out of his legs and his passes lose some of their speed and precision. In retrospect, I might better have chosen a recently retired quarterback such as Y.A. Tittle. But John was 34 when I talked to him and I figured he might be "slowing down" after 11 pro seasons. (The 1967–68 season proved how wrong I was.)

I had been told that John was not easy to interview. (It is difficult to refer to John Unitas by his last name. Unitas certainly is not a difficult name to pronounce, and his personality doesn't seem to call for the informality of first names. But both face-to-face and in sports pages he is frequently called John or Johnny or Johnny U. This is a minor phenomenon which I can't explain.) A Baltimore sportswriter who'd interviewed him many times said, "He wants to be helpful, but he's just naturally terse of speech. No question ever leads to the next. There's never any discussion of a subject." I remembered the sportswriter's remarks as I was having lunch in Westminster and I wondered if Unitas would live up to this advance billing.

In the afternoon, the dormitory lawn had turned into a crowd scene. Scores of people had gathered, all waiting to see Johnny Unitas, talk to him, obtain his autograph. He sat on the dormitory steps with a couple of other players, signing autographs and posing for pictures with young boys who were obviously getting the thrill of their lives. Eventually he spotted me and said, "Go on up to my room. I'll be along in a few minutes."

His room did not reveal much about him. The open closet contained a few items of apparel, sweaters, sport shirts and a suit, nearly all blue in color. There was a blue suitcase and a couple of magazines, *U. S. News and World Report* and *Sport,* which I read to pass the time.

Eventually he came in, took his playbook from the desk and flopped on the lower bunk. "You don't mind if I study while we talk," he said. He really didn't ask – he announced. The truth is, I did mind. I found it disconcerting to talk to a man who was scribbling notes and numbers while answering my questions. I never did get used to it, but I must admit his studying didn't hinder him in replying to my questions. I guess that being able to do more than one thing at a time is a good thing in quarterbacks.

Unitas is six feet tall and weighs around 195. He has a well-proportioned frame, with muscular arms, heavy shoulders and sturdy legs. Without having an overpowering physique, he looks solid and hard. His face is triangular-shaped, his eyes pale blue, his dark blond hair crew cut. He was wearing a blue golf shirt, dark blue pants, and loafers which he removed before dropping on the bed.

For the first half of the interview I wished I'd listened to my sportswriter friend. John was extremely difficult to draw out. I'd ask a question. He'd hesitate, think about his answer (scribbling all the while), then reply—briefly, right to the point, totally positive. He was devoid of equivocation. He hardly ever used a qualifying word like "rather," or "almost" or "sometimes."

For example, I asked him if he felt any effects of age. "No, I'm just as quick as I've ever been. My speed is just the same." That settled it. He hadn't said he was "just about" as fast or indicated any doubt about his ability. I tried to move him from this position by asking a series of questions: Could he throw as far? Was his release time a little slower? Were certain plays harder to execute? Yes. No. No. I tried a new tack. What did he think caused players to quit?

"I don't know. I suspect a lot of guys quit too early. They still have ability, but they tire of playing, have other interests, dislike the effort involved in staying in shape. There might be many reasons."

I tried another approach: When he did begin to feel his age, which of his faculties would be affected first? He thought about that awhile, or maybe he was just thinking about the playbook. After 10 or 15 seconds, he said, "I don't know. I've always heard the legs are first to go. I suspect this is true in baseball and basketball. A player can still shoot baskets, but he can't get around the floor quickly enough or jump as high. It's different with a quarterback. Ability to run isn't so important. Everybody knows I never could run. What matters is knowing the plays and throwing the ball according to the way the defenses are set. Old legs shouldn't affect this."

I tried one more time. How would he know when it was time to quit? He smiled and said, "People will let you know. There's no shortage of experts. People who never picked up a football in their lives can tell you exactly what you ought to do." His tone as he said it was a mixture of bitterness, condescension and tolerance.

That was my discussion of the effects of aging with Johnny Unitas. I now had to find something else to ask him about – and I had no idea what. I floundered around trying to find something to get him interested in. I asked if his friendship with Berry had helped make them a great passing combination.

"You can't carry personal feelings onto the field. If he's a good man, you use his ability, whatever you might think of him personally."

Did he ever think of retiring?

"No, barring injury, I can play several years. I certainly want to play. I'm enjoying every phase of the game." (A few weeks later, Unitas signed a three-year contract at a salary of $375,000.)

Did he weary of the training and conditioning?

"No, I don't mind the work. I enjoy it and do it because I want to. If you put 100 per cent into anything, you get 100 per cent out of it."

I shot questions at him, and got those brief, positive, unrevealing answers.

Looking back over his career, what gave him the greatest satisfaction?

"I never look back. Maybe when I'm 65 or 70 I will, but that's some time away."

How long had he been interested in football?

"Since the eighth grade."

Where had he grown up?

"Pittsburgh."

Had he played other sports?

"All sports."

Why had he chosen football?

"I just liked it more. Actually I was a better basketball player in high school."

I was getting nowhere. I felt like a mouse running a maze.

I asked him if the widely publicized story about his signing with the Colts was true. Supposedly, Unitas had been a highly regarded quarterback at the University of Louisville. He had been scouted by a number of pro teams and drafted by the Los Angeles Rams, who promptly traded him to the Pittsburgh Steelers. After a try-out, he was released. He spent the next year playing semi-pro ball. Then Baltimore, desperate for a quarterback to back up George Shaw, had invested 60 cents in a phone call to Pittsburgh and recruited Unitas. Soon after, Shaw broke his ankle and Unitas got his chance.

John said the story was approximately true, but added a few details. "After the Steelers released me, I received a telegram from Paul Brown, who was coaching the Cleveland Browns at that time. I talked with him by phone and he explained his situation. Otto Graham had retired and Cleveland wasn't too happy with its quarterbacks. But Brown talked Graham into coming out of retirement for one more season. Brown wanted me to sit out that season and sign with them the next. I said I would. I sat out the 1954 season. Then Weeb Ewbank, who was coaching Baltimore, called. He needed a quarterback badly and asked me to come. I told him about my conversation with Paul Brown, but the Colts sent me a contract for $1,000. It was a bird in hand so I signed it and came to Baltimore."

Had he been discouraged during that year off?

"No, I was full of confidence. I knew I could do well if I only got the chance. It was only a matter of time till I got that chance."

That topic exhausted, I tried to go back to his football origins. Had his father encouraged him?

"My father died when I was five. My mother worked very hard to support my brother, two sisters and me. I didn't see much of her. So I did most everything on my own. It made me self-reliant. My whole family is that way."

Had he had unusual success in football to encourage him?

"I never played on a championship team till I got to the Colts. I played at St. Justin High in Pittsburgh and at Louisville. We played a tough schedule and beat some good teams, but we were never champions."

In the next several minutes of intensive questioning, I learned that he had weighed only 135 pounds in high school, but gained 50 pounds in college without performing any special exercises; that his major in college had been physical education and economics but his only ambition was to play football; that he and Baltimore's All-Pro defensive back Bobby Boyd were building a restaurant in Baltimore; that he didn't play football for money. "A fellow has to want to play to be any good at it. There are lots of ways to make money without breaking your head. A fellow would be stupid to play for money."

To say that this was an unhappy interview so far is no criticism of Johnny Unitas. He was simply terse and to the point, answering my questions in a direct, matter-of-fact way. If it did nothing else, John's casual response gave me a strong impression of the kind of man he was. I felt that, to an amazing degree, he was without what psychologists would call insecurity. He was a rare, rare man – extraordinarily confident and positive. For this reason, my questions implying that he might have doubts about his ability or physical condition after 11 pro seasons struck no responsive cord. He had no doubts at all.

His total security had another effect. Johnny Unitas was friendly, courteous, highly likable – but somewhat aloof and, therefore, unloquacious. I suspected it would be very difficult to know him really well, to know his thoughts, worries, problems.

It was only when I remembered Berry's suggestion and asked John when he released the ball in a pass play that he came to life. His pencil stopped scribbling. "It all depends," he said. "In a long pass there are many factors – who the receiver is, his speed, field position, the defensive man's position and speed, whether I wish the pass to have a high trajectory or low, the play I've called in the huddle, the down, the score — many, many factors. Naturally, I'd like to get the ball to the receiver as quickly as possible, but the position of the defender may force a change in that.

"The receiver's problem is to get open so I can throw to him. He may not be able to, so then I'll have to go to another receiver who is open. All of this depends upon the type of defense we're up against. If it is a difficult or unexpected one, we have to change our plans and make adjustments."

I asked him to suppose the receiver was open. When did he throw the ball?

"I try to throw when the receiver is even with the defender. I have to figure he will beat the defender. I throw to an approximate spot based upon his direction, his speed and how far I can throw."

Encouraged, I asked John much the same questions I had asked Berry about the need for practice: "The problem is to find enough time," he said. "There are many pass patterns to be run with many different receivers, and I can only make so many throws."

I said it sounded like work, and he replied, "The good Lord is the only one who doesn't have to work too hard."

Unitas finally began to talk in earnest when I asked him what abilities had made him an outstanding quarterback.

"There are lots of men who are better passers than I, and heaven knows, there are many who run better. I think there are better ball handlers, too, many of them. My greatest ability lies in knowledge of defenses, recognition of defenses in a game, and in making adjustments to offset defenses."

In a way this statement was not surprising, for the ability of Johnny Unitas to identify and take advantage of defensive weaknesses has been reported many times. Yet if Johnny Unitas is not the greatest passing quarterback who ever played football, who is? At the start of the 1967 season, Unitas held the current record for most yards gained, passing, in a lifetime, 29,593 (breaking Y. A. Tittle's mark of 28,339) and after two regular season games, he passed the 30,000-yard mark. He held the record for most touchdown passes in a lifetime with 232, again breaking Tittle's record of 212. He had gained over 300 yards by passing in 21 different games for another record. He had thrown touchdown passes in 47 consecutive games, a record. At the start of the season he had completed 2,006 lifetime passes, ranking second to Tittle's 2,118. In the sixth game of the 1967 season, John took command of this record, too.

Statistics certainly do not tell the whole story. During his years with the Colts, John had been blessed with great receivers in Berry, John Mackey, Billy Orr, Lenny Moore and others. It is significant that, except during his early years when Alan Ameche was fullback, the Colts never had a strong running game, which meant the team stressed passing. And Baltimore has had a consistently powerful team that has included excellent pass blockers. But this is quibbling. On the basis of year-in, year-out performance over many seasons, Johnny Unitas is the greatest passer who ever played professional football. Therefore I thought it noteworthy that he played down his ability to throw the ball.

To Unitas, though, his answer was entirely reasonable. What fascinated him was the art of quarterbacking, and in his mind this encompassed far more than just throwing — as I would soon learn. Now, talking not about Johnny Unitas, but about quarterbacking, Unitas' terseness disappeared. He became an outgoing, even garrulous man.

"A team will have many defensive formations," he began, "but for the most part they will use 16 or 17 most frequently. We study these. We take the films of opponents' games and the coaching staff goes over them with us in detail. Scouts give us a great deal of information. Then I take the films home. I have a projector and screen and I study these films by the hour. In this way I learn to spot each defensive formation. I look for keys to the defensive plays. It might be the arrangement of the linebackers or backs. The defense, of course, is trying to conceal its intent, but if you study enough you can spot idiosyncrasies on the part of a linebacker, for example, which will tip off whether he intends to blitz or fall back to cover a pass. And sometimes I detect a pattern to the defenses. On third down and short yardage, the defense may usually set for a running play or a short pass or what have you. Or, they may frequently blitz in certain situations. There could be many patterns."

John then began to talk about offenses.

"On the basis of our studies, we develop offensive plans based upon the expected defenses. We stress certain plays we think will work. But we get into the game and the opponent has a different set of defenses. The opponents aren't stupid. They've looked at your films. They know your strengths and weaknesses. They've figured out what you are apt to do and made plans to stop you. So it may take awhile in a game to figure out these new defenses, pinpoint a weakness and set up a pattern of plays. Each quarterback has to set up his own pattern that gets things going his way. This is why shuttling quarterbacks doesn't work very well. When the new quarterback comes in, he has to start over with his own pattern.

"In the huddle I call the play I think is right. I may be part of my pattern to set up a later play, or it may be the one to go for a touchdown. But I have to do what I think is right. I'm the one out on the field. I have to call the play. If it doesn't work and the coach or writers or fans or anyone else think I should have called another play, they can pick up the football and go right into the game."

I asked if that attitude applied to his coach, Don Shula.

"Yes sir! If he doesn't like the plays I call, he has another quarterback sitting right there on the bench. He is paying him good money. He can send him in."

What if the coach sends in a play?

"Look, the coach doesn't know what the defense is going to do. He's not out on the field. If I run the coach's play, and it is the wrong one for that particular defense, he'll chew me out. He expects me to know. I'm supposed to be the brains.

"In the huddle I call a play based upon – oh, I don't know how many factors – the down, the yardage, the score, my pattern and the expected defensive formation. We get to the line of scrimmage and the defense has called an entirely different formation. My play is all wrong. It'll never work, so I 'check off.' I call another play at the line of scrimmage based upon the defenses, but as I'm calling it, the defense guesses what I'm doing and shifts into a new formation. The play I just called is all wrong and it doesn't work.

"Or, we run a play that should work, except that the defensive back made a mistake. He didn't go where he was supposed to go according to his own play. But his mistake put him in precisely the right position to mess up our play – and he walks off the field a hero. You'd be amazed how often that happens. Or, suppose something like this occurs: Berry is the number one receiver, but he's covered. The number two or three receiver has to recognize what has happened and make adjustments while the play is in progress. Or, maybe Berry makes adjustments himself, changing his pattern to go inside instead of outside or whatever. I have to adjust, too, and anticipate the changes the receivers will make."

John Unitas was talking about an immensely complicated and brainy game. A play called in the huddle might be checked off at the line of scrimmage, then be thwarted by a last-second defensive adjustment or player error, so that the offensive team would have to improvise changes during the few seconds the play was in progress. For these in-play adjustments to work, a team would have to play and practice together so long that the players were almost able to read each other's minds.

I said professional football sounded like a highly mobile, greatly accelerated chess game played for very high stakes.

He agreed. "The other guy is out there to beat you. He's getting paid to win, and he gets chewed out for mistakes just like you do. He's not stupid. He's studying you every bit as hard as you are studying him. If you fall into a pattern of offensive plays so that he can suspect the play you're going to call, he'll clobber you. He may do it anyhow by simply overpowering you physically. There's nothing you can do about that. No one is perfect. Mistakes are made. I think a player can be excused for a physical error, but a mental error can never be excused. There is no room for the guy who doesn't use his head."

I said it sounded to me that against a good defensive team a play had about a fifty-fifty chance of working.

"I don't know the percentage," he said, "but it is certain that nothing will work all the time. That's why I have to do what I think is right. The alleged experts in the stands forget that the other team has a lot to say about whether a play works. I've said it right on television that if the people of Baltimore don't like what I do, they can get another boy."

I asked him if other quarterbacks didn't study defenses as he did.

"Sure they do, but some pick it up faster than others."

He got off the bunk, then, and said he had to go to practice. The interview was over, to my regret, and we walked out of the dormitory together. Outside another crowd of fans waited for John's autograph. Smiling, he obliged, scribbling his name as he made his way slowly toward the campus locker room.

To me, John Unitas was a very special man. He had no doubts about what he was doing or why. He had no second thoughts, no misgivings. He did not hesitate, seek advice, form a consensus. He gave not one iota of consideration to the opinions others might have of what he did, except to be annoyed by them. Most men doubt themselves, question their ability, worry about their mistakes and about the attitudes of others. Such men become leaders in many fields because they have courage to make a decision, carry it out and endure their own doubts, worries and self-criticism.

Johnny Unitas seemed to bypass this process. He was totally self-confident. If it was third down and 23 yards to go with time for only one play in a championship game, I'm certain he would have no doubts about what play to call. He wouldn't say in the huddle, "Okay, fellows, what should we do now?" Without hesitation, he'd call the play he thought most likely to work.

If it didn't he'd feel – but let him describe his feelings. I posed approximately this situation and asked Unitas how he felt as he walked off the field, the picture of dejection. He said, "Look, the other guy's getting paid to beat you. Somebody has to lose." I asked him if he wasn't upset. He shook his head no. Didn't he feel anything? He said, "Of course, I'm not happy to lose. Who would be? Sure I'm upset. But I've never been upset over anything more than five minutes in my life. It happened, so it happened, so forget it and go on to something else."

At the end of the 1966 season, he'd had a couple of poor games, notably in the All-Pro game. This didn't set him to wondering if he was over the hill. He had a bad day, so what else was new?

It is this self-confidence, this lack of insecurity, that makes John Unitas the great team leader he's known to be. Football is the ultimate challenge to Unitas, the demanding crucible in which his confidence and abilities are tested. Winning is satisfying to him, I'm sure, but the thrill for him is in outwitting an opponent who is trying to outwit him. In a close game, he is forced dozens of times to call on his innermost resources, take great risks, blend with great precision his physical skill and mental cunning.

What my conversation with Unitas did was to make me, for the first time in my life, wish I had played football. I'd always thought of it as a game in which big guys knocked each other down in a contest of physical power that was exciting to watch but must be painful to endure. Unitas let me in on a very different sport—an immensely brainy game. I realized that as the professionals play it, physical prowess is the common denominator. The physical edge, if any, must be slight. The difference between winning and losing is how intelligently the players perform.

It was obvious, after the interview (without knowing how well he would perform in the coming season), that talking to Johnny about the problems of aging was a waste of time. He will be around for a while. He loves the sport. It's a tremendous challenge to him, a game combining chess, checkers, Monopoly, hide and seek and a few others. I wondered how football had ever developed from its original knockdown, runover style into the intricate, sophisticated duel it has become. I wondered, too, if any other activity designed by man is such a blend of maximum physical ability, precision, strategy, innovation and old-fashioned riverboat gambling. I couldn't think of any.

JOE DON LOONEY

Joe Don Looney

"If I had it to do over a hundred times, I'd do the same."

I LEFT the Colts camp and drove about 50 miles north to Carlisle, Pennsylvania, where the Washington Redskins were in training at Dickinson College. The man I was going to see was Joe Don Looney. I had chosen Looney as Raymond Berry's opposite, and finding a man to fit this category was difficult. Berry was a player of limited physical ability who became a star. I wanted to interview a player of great physical ability who had flopped. The comparison, I thought, might be interesting.

But who? I prepared a long list. It seemed that I could select almost any highly-touted, first-draft-choice college quarterback. They are signed for huge bonuses, receive great publicity and then usually become invisible on the bench. But a rookie quarterback didn't quite seem to fit. A quarterback in professional football is a special person.

He must be able to pass, true, but that is the least of what he must do. He needs the indefinable quality of leadership and, most of all, ability to "read" defenses and call plays, a talent that apparently comes only with experience. A rookie quarterback is almost never an immediate success. Most have to undergo a long apprenticeship. Besides, I felt there was no way for me to judge whether the young quarterback really had outstanding ability. He might just be the product of a great publicity build-up.

The more I thought about it, the more I wanted a player of unquestioned physical ability who had failed because of his own shortcomings. These I thought would probably be in the areas of concentration, effort, discipline and, to be blunt about it, character. The problem was that the man had to realize his situation and be willing to talk about it. I didn't think there were many players like this who would.

I talked to several people and the list, still largely of quarterbacks, grew, but none seemed an ideal choice. Then one day I mentioned my problem to an executive of the National Football League. "I can think of one man right away who would be ideal for you," he said, "but I don't know if he'd do it." I asked who. "Joe Don Looney." Of course. A first draft choice of the New York Giants, traded as "a bad apple" to the Baltimore Colts, then to the Detroit Lions, Joe Don Looney had been on the sports pages frequently, as reporters recapitulated and analyzed his bumpy career. I asked if he was still in the league. "Oh, yes, he's with Washington. In fact, it may ruin your story because it looks like he might make it there." Not at all. It would be even better if the player could talk not only about his mistakes but about how he had corrected them.

I called Joe Blair, the Redskins publicity director, and explained why I wanted to interview Looney. "I'll ask him," he said, "but you should know that when Joe came with us, we all agreed he was making a fresh start. There would be no discussion of the past. It's worked fine and Joe is doing very well with us." I said I had no interest in the past except as a contrast with the present and the future. Looney agreed to see me.

I met Joe Don Looney as he emerged from the shower. I didn't seek this informality, but when I walked into the Dickinson College dormitory and asked for Looney, someone pointed to a doorway. It turned out to be the bathroom, and there was Looney, wearing only a towel. He had a formidable physique. It was not that he was so big. At six-feet-one, and 220 pounds, he would be dwarfed by a 275-pound, six-foot-five lineman. But he had phenomenal musculature, bulging arms, immense shoulders, a bear's chest and legs like telephone poles. He look like a Charles Atlas advertisement, the antithesis of the 97-pound weakling. Whatever lack of discipline he might or might not have in perfecting his football techniques, it was certain that he had spent long hours lifting weights and performing isometric exercises.

He pointed out his room and said he'd be along as soon as he shaved. Looney's room looked as if a scrimmage had been held there. A great litter was scattered about. One of the two bunks was neat enough, although it would hardly pass an Army inspection, but the other sagged under an immense pile of clothes, shoes and other gear. In the corner was a portable record player and a cardboard whiskey box filled with albums, mostly show tunes and jazz. The dresser was piled with letters and magazines. Pasted to the mirror were several snapshots of an attractive blonde girl.

The room contained a significant amount of reading material: *The Great Quotations,* compiled by George Seldes; *Six Weeks to Words of Power* by Wilfred Funk; *Pragmatism and Other Essays* by William James; the current issue of *TV Guide;* and an issue of the *National Enquirer,* the misadventures of a Hollywood starlet emblazoned on its cover. Looney certainly had diverse literary tastes.

He entered, still draped in the towel and took note of the shambles in the room, saying, "Got to clean this up. I'm living like a rat."

Looney has black eyes, short black hair combed forward and a head that seems too small for what must be a size 20 neck. His shaving had been confined to his cheeks and neck. His upper lip and chin were graced with a fine, one-day stubble. He was starting a mustache and beard.

As he dabbed himself with cologne and went about the business of dressing, we talked. Looney quickly conveyed two things about himself. The first was intensity. It came from his bright, burning eyes, his physique, his quick, decisive movements, and most of all, from his manner of speaking. He was extremely earnest. There was no doubt of his great conviction about everything he said. At the same time, he was volatile. He had so many ideas, such a wealth of opinions. A happy wisecrack would be followed by cynical bitterness. He would be humble one moment and arrogant the next. He would make what seemed to be an eminently reasonable statement, then follow it with a notion that sounded plain cockeyed to me. And all the moods and attitudes were conveyed with such intensity that I felt as if I were striking matches on top of a tank of gasoline.

None of this is reported as criticism. Joe Don Looney was a fascinating man to be with. I liked him. His personality was simply the opposite of Raymond Berry's placid serenity.

I asked Looney how he felt and what he anticipated for the season.

"I was bothered all last year by a whiplash injury, but I've been taking treatments and it's much better," he said. "I've been working out with the first team, although I haven't been allowed to do any contact scrimmaging yet. But I expect to be in there for the first exhibition game. I think it'll be a good season. This is a great team. We could go all the way."

I told him my conversation with Joe Blair and said I just had to talk to him about the past. He said that would be all right.

"I grew up in Fort Worth, Texas," he began. "I was a skinny kid, but I played all kinds of sports. I can't say I had any great yearning to play football, but I did go out for the team my junior year in high school. Made the B team. I was on the varsity as a halfback my senior year. That was Paschal High School in Fort Worth.

"After high school I enrolled in the University of Texas, but not to play football. I had no football scholarship. I hadn't tried for one. I only weighed 170 pounds, which wasn't big enough, and I wasn't dreadfully interested. My father had played end at TCU. He had been on a national championship team in 1938, so I always felt that if I did play football it would be at TCU.

"I pledged a fraternity right off and soon realized it was not for me. I couldn't stand all the phony snobs and I was quite unhappy. At the end of the first semester I realized I wanted to play football, but I'd already messed myself up. I was just 18 and I was a dumb jerk. My grades weren't any good and I was off the team before I ever got on it.

"The next year, that would be my sophomore year, I enrolled in Camden Junior College in Lawton, Oklahoma. By this time I was 185 pounds and fast. I could do 60 yards in 6.3 wearing a track suit. We had a great team and ended up as National Junior College champions. I was offered football scholarships from all over the country. I accepted an offer from the University of Oklahoma."

"Why Oklahoma?" I asked.

"Oh, Oklahoma was a football power. Bud Wilkinson was the coach and he was a great man. I figured this was the best place for me. I played there my junior year and did okay. I did most of the punting and was selected on a few All-American teams."

He did "okay," indeed. He ranked fifth in the nation in rushing with 852 yards and was the number one punter with an average of 43.4 yards per kick.

At this point I was noting the similarities between Berry's career and Looney's. Both were from Texas. Both had been too small to play on major teams. Each had gone to junior colleges and excelled, attacting the attention of big-time coaches. The similarities ended there.

"I was dismissed from the team after the third game of my senior year. I got into a fight with an assistant coach. It doesn't really matter what the fight was over, but I was suspended from the team for disciplinary reasons. I cooled off and realized I'd made a mistake. I went to Wilkinson and said I was sorry and that I'd like to return to the team. He said he appreciated my attitude and bygones would be bygones. Two days later he announced that I had been dismissed from the team. He said the team had voted me out, but I know they didn't. To the day I die I'll say I never should have been dismissed. I know a lot of things I've never talked about and maybe never will, but all I know is I never should have been kicked off the team."

Looney was reluctant to talk about the Oklahoma incident. He would only add, rather cryptically, "I was upset to be booted off the team, and yet I was kind of happy. It was a bad situation, and I was glad to be out of it, even if it meant not playing football."

I did not press him for details. Looney clearly did not want to talk about the episode. But the dismissal was strange. Wilkinson was quoted as saying Looney was a "bad influence" on the team, indifferent about practicing and following rules. Wilkinson said the team voted him out. Looney denied this. It seemed to me that most college coaches would put up with a certain amount of trouble from a player who had gained 852 yards the year before. In any event, Looney kept his football scholarship and got his degree from the university.

Whatever the real story is, as a result of the incident, Looney was branded a hard-to-handle player. For this reason, sportswriters and fans alike were surprised when, after the 1963 season, the New York Giants selected Looney as their first draft choice. That year the Giants had won the Eastern Division title, then lost to the Chicago Bears in the title game, 14–10. The Giants were looking for a big, fast running back. But so were a number of teams. Washington, making the third selection, chose Charley Taylor from Arizona, who had gone on to stardom. The Colts selected Marv Woodson of Indiana. Pittsburgh drafted Paul Martha of Pittsburgh University. The Cleveland Browns made an enviable selection in Paul Warfield of Ohio State. The Giants, choosing 12th, picked Looney. There were still a number of top backs around. The Colts selected Tony Lorick of Arizona on the second round. He has been a standout. The Giants' second round choice was Steve Thurlow of Yale, who has done well in the NFL.

When sportswriters asked Jim Lee Howell about the selection of Looney, a player who had sat out most of that college season, Howell, the Giants' director of player personnel, said, "He was the best college back I saw by far in 1962." Tom Brookshier, a scout for the Philadelphia Eagles, commented, "If they can get him to

Yankee Stadium, he'll play a lot of football for the Giants."

The Giants got Looney to Yankee Stadium all right, but he didn't play a lot of football. He was traded to Baltimore at the start of the season, despite the fact it is traditional for a first draft choice to at least make the team, if not play regularly.

Looney explained what happened. "I didn't know anything about pro football. I'd never even seen a game. I had no idea what being a first draft choice meant. I thought the sun rose and set in Norman, Oklahoma. When I went to New York, I was immediately unhappy. I didn't like the city and, with a few exceptions, I didn't like the players. You see, I didn't have the right attitude, nor did I want to. Anything that happens to any New York athlete is blown up out of all proportion in the press and sent out all over the country on wire services. The players get big reputations which they really don't deserve and this affects everyone. If I acted like the rest of these guys, I should have felt and acted as though I were great. Step aside, man, I'm the number one rookie. I know I should have felt that way, but I couldn't. These fellows were just like the fraternity boys in Texas. Look at me, I'm a New York Giant. I'm the world's greatest. Didn't the papers just say it?" He made a gesture of total disgust. "They're a bunch of bums. I asked to be traded."

And so he was traded, along with his reputation as a temperamental, hard-to-handle player.

"It was a blessing to be traded to the Colts. It was an honor to play with that team. I was happy to make any small contribution I could. I mostly played on the kickoff and punt return teams, because the Colts already had four good running backs in Lenny Moore, Tony Lorick, Jerry Hill and Tom Matte. They were way ahead of me. I didn't even learn the Colts plays until the second game, and then I pulled a thigh muscle. Besides, the Colts won 11 straight that year on their way to the Western Division title. Why break up a winning combination?"

Looney was traded to the Detroit Lions for the 1965 season, but, he said, not because he didn't get along with the Colts. "Harry Gilmer, the Lions' coach, said he asked for me and I believe him. After all, he traded Dennis Gaubatz, one of the best linebackers in the league, for me.

"I started off in Detroit like a house afire. My exhibition season was as good as anybody's. Detroit had a great defense, but a poor offense, and I felt I was really helping the team. But I forgot what it was that I'd come to Detroit for. It got to be less and less football and more and more having fun. Detroit was a real swinging town. I'd walk into a bar and everybody'd start buying me drinks. It seemed everybody wanted to invite Looney to their parties and I did my best to make them all. Then every Monday a couple of other fellows and I threw a party. It was a real blast with lots of booze and girls. I got so I lived more for the Monday night parties than the game that made them possible.

"In the eighth game of the season I suffered a whiplash injury. I pinched a nerve in my neck and had excruciating headaches. Everytime I'd hit the line it felt like the top of my skull flew off. Soon I started flinching and hesitating, and I wasn't any good at all.

"I still had the headaches at the start of the 1966 season, but that really wasn't my problem. The Lions were a funny team. It had to be handled right and Gilmer was having his problems. He and I had an argument, and I was traded to Washington after the third game."

I asked what the Redskins had traded for him.

"A draft choice." He smiled. "About the 20th, I think. My price was going down."

I asked what he and Gilmer had argued about.

"Let's just say we both made mistakes. I wasn't doing my own thinking. I was very much influenced by the attitude on the team. I got to thinking people owed me things when they didn't."

I asked how the season went in Washington.

"I started one game, but my head still hurt terribly. I got down on myself and my attitude was very bad. I would have quit football if I could have figured another way to earn a living. As it was I just tried to see how many different girls I could date."

Looney, I reflected, was sketching with brutal honesty a portrait of a young man squandering his talents. What I wondered, would cause the conversion I knew had occurred?

Looney supplied the answer immediately. "In December of that year [1966] I was in New York and I met a girl. Right away I knew this was the one. I took her to Fort Worth on the second date to meet my family, and we were married in April. She is a real fine girl, much smarter than I am, a real student. Getting married did everything for me. All of a sudden I wanted to settle down, raise kids and amount to something.

"I started thinking about someone other than myself, and I began to take stock of myself. I realized I was all messed up. If I didn't really want to do something, I'd start to feel sorry for myself and think up excuses for not doing it. And you know how easy it is to think of excuses. Gilmer was mistreating me. Gilmer didn't do such and such. Why should I do all that tiresome practice. Maybe I'd get traded to Los Angeles and be a big star in the movies. I'm a big dreamer. I got a real imagination. I wanted to be President and play football at the same time. Or, I'd get a big urge to scale the Alps. Or, I'd want to buy a boat and sail around the world. I still might do that – after I prove I can play football.

"I've thought about all the mistakes I've made and now I realize what's important. I want to play football. I don't want to be the infamous Joe Looney. I want to be the famous Joe Looney. I want people to talk about what Looney is, not what he could be. I want to show people just how good a football player I am."

He was on his feet now, pacing the cluttered room, extremely intense in word and gesture.

"Look, I'm an aware guy. I know what's going on in the world. There are things I want to say. I'm interested in politics, for example. Take Goldwater. He was a real man. How the voters could turn him down and put that weakling in the White House I'll never figure out. But I got to make something out of myself before anyone will listen to me. Who wants to listen to a guy who lives in a shack?"

He sat down and talked more calmly. "I'm still Looney. Like my wife says, I can never see anything gray. Everything is either white or black, good or bad to me. When I work, I work. When I play, I play. There is never any middle ground. Well, I'm here to work. I'm going to be a football player. I've quit drinking, for example, and I've stopped second-guessing the coach. You know, these training camps are tough. It's a dull life and you're worked to death. Always before I'd think: why do I have to do all this running or tackling or blocking exercises? Now I say the coach must have some reason. If this is what he wants, I'll do it. I have all the respect in the world for Otto Graham [the Redskins' coach]. He is a real man and the most honest guy I've ever met. He talks to you straight. You know exactly what he means. I sure do want to play for him. And this team will surprise a lot of people."

He stopped talking for a moment, then almost as an afterthought added, "Everybody talks about Looney's potential. What's potential? It and fifteen cents will get you a cup of coffee most anywhere."

It was late so I left, after we agreed to continue the next day. I was pleased. I felt I had what I came for: some insight into why and how Raymond Berry would overcome limited physical assets to become a star, while Joe Don Looney, with great abilities, was struggling to find himself. Berry had desire, single-mindedness, discipline, the willingness to pay any price to achieve his goal. Looney had lacked these qualities, it seemed, though now he sounded like a man who at least knew what his problem was. I, for one, hoped he did.

When I came back the next afternoon, I encountered a somewhat different Looney, although it took me awhile to realize it. I began by asking him to forget about modesty and give me a realistic self-appraisal of his football talents.

"I have good speed. I'm an elusive runner, yet I can hit with power. I can catch passes, so I'm both an inside and outside threat. I'm a better than adequate blocker. My problem is lack of experience. I had only one year of high school football and two years of college. My three years as a pro really add up to approximately one year. I've a lot to learn. I'm not good at following my blockers. I tend to go it on my own. In a word, I don't run smart."

I told him that I hoped he made it big this season. I said I was sure that if he did, football fans all over the country would be glad for him. Everyone loved a winner, especially if he overcame adversity to become one. His next comment surprised me.

"I'm not dreadfully concerned with what people think. Every man ought to think for himself. Each person ought to march to the beat of a different drum. I'm a loner, always have been, and nobody likes the man who stands alone. People think that as long as you do what the other guy does a crowd makes it right. But it doesn't. You have to think for yourself and do what you think is right. Yet going along with the crowd creeps up on you. The dove flies with crows and thinks he's black.

"I don't know. I might do something a little different. I live in this country and I have an obligation for the military service. But that is a rotten war in Vietnam. I don't know, I might do like Cassius Clay and go to jail rather than serve. I got an obligation, but I also have a choice if things get too unreasonable for me."

I shook my head. I didn't seem to be hearing right. This wasn't the same fellow I'd listened to the night before.

"Sure, I want to be a football player, but I don't see why I have to sacrifice everything to become a star. Since I married I've changed my way of living, but because I wanted to, not because I felt I ought to. I feel that if what a man is doing is important, he ought to stand up and be counted."

He launched into a discussion of General Billy Mitchell, the Army officer who had been court-martialed in the 1920's when he fought for the concept of air power. Somehow, just about the time I thought I had grasped Joe Don Looney, he had vaporized and reappeared in a new form. I got him back on the subject by asking him to tell me again about his troubles the second year in Detroit.

"I was running with the second team. Amos Marsh was first string halfback and having a very good year. After the second exhibition game, the backfield coach came to me and said, 'Looney, you're now first string. You beat out Amos.'

"The next game was in Tulsa, Oklahoma, and I figured I should start. Instead, Gilmer started Amos. I asked him about it, and he said he was starting Amos because we were playing Dallas and that was Amos's old team. That just wasn't a good enough reason for me. I said it was out and out wrong and I asked to be traded. He said he wasn't going to.

"The next day Harry said he wanted to try me at fullback, because I'd never been given a chance there. Then he said that if I ever had a good game, he'd never take me out. That was good enough for me. All I needed was a chance to prove what I could do.

"It came in the third game against Atlanta. Early in the game I broke for a touchdown. Later, in a third down and six situation, I made a first down. We started driving for a touchdown — and he took me out and put in another guy. He scored the touchdown.

"I sat there and knew I couldn't play for this man. He'd said to me that he'd never take me out if I was having a good game. Well, I was and he still took me out. He told me to go back in. I told him I couldn't play for anybody who broke his word like that and refused to go back in. He blew up, suspended me and told me to get dressed."

The night before, Looney had spoken of this incident, saying, "Harry and I both made mistakes."

The next day he said: "If I had it to do over a hundred times, I'd do the same."

I asked him if he didn't feel a coach had a right to manage the team as he saw fit.

Looney was vehement. "Sure he has a right to manage. But where do my rights come in? Funny thing was that I liked Detroit. I liked the team. I even liked Harry and no one else did. The guys told me to hold on, to go along, that Gilmer wouldn't last long. But I couldn't. I'm not one of the crowd."

It seemed to me that this attitude had no relationship at all to the things said by the grimly determined young man I'd seen the night before. I didn't know what to make of him. He was so changeable. He hadn't liked the Giants because he hadn't wanted to cultivate phony arrogance. He loved Baltimore and was glad to make some small contribution to its success. In Detroit he insisted on being traded and refused to play because he was taken out of a game when he was doing well. One night he called it a mistake. The next day he'd do it over again a hundred times. It struck me that a coach would have to be a soothsayer to guess his reactions.

Had he ever had troubles with Otto Graham, I asked?

"No, I've never had any trouble. Oh, I've disagreed with him. For example, he called a particularly long practice, and I couldn't see any point in it. Then, I thought about it and I could see the point. If you are in good condition, you shouldn't mind a two-and-a-half-hour practice."

He'd flipflopped again, back to sweet reasonableness.

"Look," he said, "I'd like to knock this off. There's an exercise room downstairs and I'd like to work out an hour or so before practice."

I said it didn't look to me like he needed any more muscles.

"They're big enough, but I got to make them strong."

Looney was starting his fourth season in the NFL. In his first three seasons he contributed very little to four different teams, but so great was his potential that he did not lack opportunity to prove himself.

It was difficult to know what to make of him. A first impression was that he lacked discipline, but this could not be applied to all areas. Those tremendous muscles of his had been developed only through long hours of tiring, boring exercises. Obviously, he was able to do arduous routine tasks if he put his mind to it.

If he put his mind to it. Maybe that was at least part of Looney's difficulty. I knew that successful athletes believed in the need to control the mind, in order to concentrate on the playing situation, whether it was a six-foot putt, a foul shot, a pitched ball or a sweep around left end. Many of the athletes I would speak to confirmed this, saying that the most difficult thing was to close the mind to distractions and concentrate on the immediate situation.

Looney appeared woefully inept at this. He had a quick, agile mind that overflowed with thoughts and ideas. He was a perceptive person, intelligent, informed. These qualities, admirable in themselves, combined with an intense and volatile nature, must have made the reining in of his mind and emotions more difficult for Looney than for other men. But Looney was a likable guy. He was only 24. It was not unreasonable to expect that he would conquer himself and become the star player he wanted to be.

Two months after I talked to Looney, he was released by the Redskins. Newspapers reported he had not spoken to Don Doll, the offensive backfield coach, in three weeks. He was playing out his option so he could leave the team at the end of the season. His sideline indifference when not in action did not please Otto Graham. When Looney skipped two practices because of headaches, he was let go.

I was saddened by the news.

VINCE PROMUTO

65
JP

Vince Promuto

"If we really work, really drive ourselves to our utter limits, we accomplish things we never thought possible."

VINCE PROMUTO, the right guard of the Washington Redskins, looked tough. If he ever gave up football, he could consider a career as a movie "heavy." He had a large head, dominated by the biggest jaw I ever saw on a human being. I was willing to bet he used two fresh blades every day just shaving his fortress of a chin. His jaw was so big it made his head and brow look pinched, although I'm sure he wore an oversized hat.

But Promuto did not act tough. He had a shy smile, soft brown eyes and a gentle voice. He was six-feet-one, 245 pounds, with a barrel chest and arms and legs to fit it. Promuto was big all over. But he did not have Joe Don Looney's flashy physique. The old pants and sweatshirt he wore did not stretch under the pressure of bulging muscles. If he were more muscular, he explained, he would be too heavy to play his position. As it is, he can run 40 yards in five flat (compared to Berry's 4.9 over the same distance).

I had come to see Vince Promuto because he was "an average player." Not average in ability or in contribution to the team — but so much is written about the stars of a team that I wondered about the less famous player who is seldom interviewed: that was the kind of "average" guy I wanted. I wanted to know: Why did he play the sport? What did he get from it?

I chose an interior offensive lineman in football because I felt that he was the least heralded player in sports. He might perform superbly, but unless he was All-Pro or close to it, he received little notice. When the offensive team was on the field, all eyes were on the backs and receivers. Only if the lineman threw a particularly conspicuous block did the sportscaster mention him. Defensive players were much more in the limelight, as they tackled, made interceptions and blitzed the quarterback. No statistics were kept for offensive linemen. There were statistics for running, for points scored, for passing and punting, for receiving and interception leaders, punt and kickoff returns, field goals and several other categories. But nobody counted how many times a lineman opened a hole for the fullback or how many seconds he protected the quarterback from a pass rush. Yet this offensive lineman was in the thick of it, getting his brains knocked out week after week. For what?

I figured almost any "average" lineman would do. Since I was going to the Redskins' camp to interview Looney, I asked Joe Blair, the publicity director, to recommend someone. "I have just the man for you," he said. "Vince Promuto, our right guard. This is his eighth season with us. He's played in a couple of Pro Bowl games, but he was never selected as an All-Pro. He's a grand guy and has a great story that's never been told." I had never heard of Vince Promuto. He sounded perfect, a good veteran performer who was unsung.

When I arrived in the Redskins camp, I discovered Looney and Promuto were close friends. In fact, I talked to Promuto in Looney's disarrayed room.

Vince Promuto made an indelible impression on me. Of all the athletes I encountered, he was the most inspiring. There was, I discovered, nothing *average* about him.

"I've never told my story," he said, "but I guess this is as good a time as any. I was born and brought up on Buhre Avenue in the Pelham Bay Park section of the Bronx. It was a Little Italy, a very tough neighborhood. The only thing that mattered among the crowd I ran around with was how tough you were. Your social stature was won with your fists, and since I was always a big kid, I had lots of social stature. A kid might be good in school or play the piano or be a fine athlete, but if he wasn't tough, he was – well, who cared about him?

"In my early teens my father talked to me about the importance of an education. He wanted me to go to Mount St. Michaels, a Catholic high school. I had never been much of a student, but, since I'd do most anything to please my father, I agreed to take the entrance test. To my surprise I was accepted. At considerable financial sacrifice, my father sent me to Mount St. Michaels with the stipulation I play football. I weighed about 200 pounds and it seemed like I ought to play, but I never had, nor did I much want to. My idea of fun was to head for the street corner. To please my father, I went to Mount St. Michaels, but I didn't go out for football.

"I did poorly in school. I couldn't even understand what the teachers were talking about. I had a 65 grade average, and I got into some trouble. The Brothers decided to kick me out of school at the end of the year. As punishment for the trouble I got into, I was ordered to stay after school every day for a month and sift dirt for the baseball field. I was on detention so long, I got to be foreman of the dirt sifting crew.

"I was sifting away on the ball diamond one spring day while the track team was practicing in another part of the athletic field. One of the guys practicing the javelin threw wildly and almost hit me in the leg. It scared me and made me mad. I picked up the javelin and threw it back at him. I guess it went over his head.

"Next thing I knew there was the track coach. He'd seen my throw. Would I like to join the track team? Well, it seemed to me that it beat sifting dirt, so I said I might as well. That was a week before the all-city track meet."

I was greatly amused, for I felt I knew what was coming. I didn't.

"I was a dumb kid. All I knew was that little neighborhood I live in. I'd never been to a track meet, and I had no idea what went on. When I arrived at the Randalls Island Stadium that Saturday, everybody was wearing flannel sweatsuits and looking very professional. I was dressed for the corner in my double saddle stitched peg pants. I didn't even have tennis shoes, let alone track shoes. I felt terribly out of place – and I was out of place.

"Angry and embarrassed, I was determined to show everyone. When my turn came, I took off my shoes and threw in my bare feet. I'd only had a week of practice, and I didn't know a thing about form, but I reared back and threw so hard I almost put out my shoulder – and came in second. I won four points for our team, and we won the track meet by three points. That was the first time in my life I'd ever heard 100 per cent of the people cheering for me. In a street fight, you know, half the people are cheering for the other guy. I went home to tell my mother about my accomplishment. She didn't know whether to believe me or not."

Promuto said that because of the track meet, he decided that there was more to high school than he realized. He buckled down, improved his grades and, because of his athletic contribution, won another year at Mount St. Michaels.

"I decided to go out for football. Oh, that was hard. I was big enough, but I knew no fundamentals. I'd never once played the game. I remember that when we did drills with the two-man tackling sled, I couldn't even hit it. I missed entirely. Everyone laughed at me and – well I guess you know how I felt. But I stayed long after everyone left and kept hitting that machine. I couldn't stand to be lousy.

"I made the team as offensive tackle, beating out a bigger man. I made honorable mention on the all-city team my junior year and all-city as a senior. What I'm really proud of is that my grade average went up 20 points, despite all the time I spent practicing football.

"I was offered football scholarships from 36 colleges, including Notre Dame and Michigan State. At the same time I was offered a career as a professional boxer, which seemed more up my alley. But the Brothers at St. Michaels wanted me to go to Holy Cross University. So I went to Worcester, Massachusetts, one Saturday to look over the campus. I had never thought about going to college. I never even knew anyone who had ever gone. I figured all colleges were alike, so I accepted the Holy Cross scholarship. My real reason for this was that I couldn't see wasting any more Saturdays looking around colleges. If you saw one you'd seen them all, or so I thought.

"I'll never forget my surprise my sophomore year. I made the football team and we played Syracuse, staying overnight on the campus. I never knew college could be like this. There were girls on campus and dating. You could dance and listen to music. You see, Holy Cross was an all male school and rather strict about rules and behavior. Lights were out at eleven o'clock every night. I had to study way past eleven just to maintain a C average. Half the time it seemed to me the professors were talking a foreign language. To get around the curfew, I'd get in bed with my books and a lamp and pull the covers over my head. One night I fell asleep. The lamp fell over and set fire to the mattress. My roommates woke up with the room full of smoke. Fortunately I wasn't burned and we doused the mattress in the shower."

Holy Cross was hardly a football power (although it

did upset Syracuse, which was a power, in two of Promuto's three varsity years) and Promuto garnered no great collegiate reputation. At best he won honorable mention on a few All-East teams. But the pros are not too impressed by reputations, and Promuto was drafted by the New York Giants on the fourth round. He was immediately traded to the Redskins for Dick Lynch, one of the game's better defensive backs.

"I came to the Redskins Training camp in 1960 and I made the starting team my first year. This wasn't saying much — we were a pretty sorry bunch.

"I had a dreadful time as a pro the first few years. I was as big as the other pros, but I was so dumb. I came to the NFL thinking all I had to do was knock the other guy down with brute strength. The defensive men made a monkey out of me. I fell for every fake. I'd charge a defensive lineman, only he wasn't there. He had faked me out and was tackling the runner or spread-eagled on top of the quarterback I was supposed to protect. I swear I would never have made any team but this one.

"You see, I didn't know any fundamentals. I hadn't learned much in high school or college. Holy Cross was a small school. It didn't have six or seven coaches like the big colleges, and I never got much instruction. Moreover, there weren't any experienced guards on this team I could learn from. One year was the longest any had been a pro. If I'd gone with a team like the Colts and sat on the bench a couple of years watching Alex Sandusky, I'd have progressed a lot faster.

"As it was, I learned everything the hard way. I just flailed away with my body, and I took an awful beating.

On the Monday after a game, I'd be so sore I couldn't be sure I'd ever move again. Not knowing how to play my position, I'd be fooled time and again. I expended at least five times as much effort to accomplish half as much. And I had no confidence. I was down on myself most of the time.

"But I stuck to it. I didn't give up, and if you do that you are bound to improve. After my first season I wasn't a rookie any more. Maybe I'd run into a first year man once in awhile, and I'd fool him for a change and know I was making a little headway."

I asked him what his strongest asset was. His immediate answer: "Hard work. Nothing I've done has been handed to me. I haven't given up once and I've earned everything."

What was he best at doing on the field? "Oh, I'm pretty good in everything and nothing great in any of them."

How did he know? "I was one of three guys selected for the Pro Bowl in 1963 and 1964. Then we get graded on every play by the coaches. Last year I averaged 87 per cent on every play over the whole season. It was my best grade ever."

Did linemen resent the publicity given to a quarterback?

"Oh, no, the quarterback is everything in football. A team could have the greatest offensive line in the world and a lousy quarterback and it would lose every game. You put Unitas behind the worst line in the world, and he'll win half your games for you."

Promuto has worked as hard off the gridiron as on — and what he's accomplished may after all be his greatest triumph.

"After I played in the Pro Bowl in California in 1964, I was talking with Mr. Edward Bennett Williams who is president of the Redskins and also one of America's best lawyers. He asked me what I did in the off-season. I told him I was a special representative for the Pepsi Cola company in Washington. It was a good job and I met lots of people. He said, 'Why don't you go to law school and become a lawyer? You won't be in the limelight, but it will help you in a business career and bring you prestige.'

"The idea of law school frightened me. I'd never been much of a student. I'd had to work hard just to get a C in college. When I finally got my sheepskin, I handed it to my father and never expected to set foot in a classroom again. But Mr. Williams' remark affected me. I was a newlywed and I was looking for security. Being a lawyer suddenly appealed to me. So without knowing anything about law school or really giving any thought to my decision, I said, 'Mr. Williams, if you'll help me get into law school, I'll quit my job and go.' He said he'd be glad to help me.

"I don't think he believed I was serious about going to law school, but I was. I went back to Washington and quit my job. That was burning all my bridges, but I knew if I didn't do it, I'd never have the courage to go. But it was also stupid. I'd have to pass a law aptitude test before a university would accept me, and I had no idea whether I had any aptitude for the law.

"Quitting my job really put Mr. Williams on the spot, and he had to do something. He helped arrange for me to take the test and, to my surprise, I did average. I was accepted at the American University School of Law in Washington.

"Before the first day of class I was a nervous wreck. Then when I walked into the classroom, there were a bunch of newspaper photographers to take my picture. That was awful. I wondered how many photographers there would be when I was kicked out of school.

"Law school was terrible. At first I didn't understand a thing, and I had been out of school so long I didn't even know how to begin to study. On top of that, there is no way to judge how well you're doing. In law school you're tested only at the end of the semester. You either pass or fail. I spent the first semester in a state of misery. Then, to my surprise, I got an A in a tough course, one of two in the class.

"I discovered in law school that I wasn't as dumb as I thought I was. It normally takes three years to earn a degree. I did it in three and a half years – and played football half the year. I graduated in the upper third of my class and made the honor list with a 1.9 average out of a possible 3.

"Going to law school taught me that lots of people have more potential than they realize. If they are willing to work hard, they can do things they never dreamed were possible. All they have to do is not be afraid to start."

Somehow, despite his origins, Vince Promuto had discovered an elemental secret of success in any endeavor. It has many names, but the simplest is *guts*.

I asked him how much money he made playing football. "A good offensive guard with a number of years' service will make between $20,000 and $30,000 a year," he said. I expressed surprise that it was so much. "Oh, yes. After all the minimum is $12,500." His football salary had enabled him to invest in a substantial home on two acres in Potomac, Maryland, a Washington suburb. Currently, he was building a stable for his Tennessee Walking Horse.

I said it seemed to me he owed a lot to football. What would he have been without it?

"At best I'd have been in my father's garbage collection business. At worst, maybe in jail. Some of my boyhood friends have gotten into trouble. I might have, too. You see, none of us respected anyone who wasn't tough. I never knew anything else, and I had no idea everyone didn't live that way. You're right. I owe everything to football."

I asked what football demanded in return.

"You have to love football. If you play, it demands primacy in your life. If, for example, I'd been forced to choose between football and law school, it would have been football. You can't play football as a second job. Take my case. I came into the league knowing nothing and learned the hard way. Gradually I developed confidence. Confidence is everything in a pro. You have to believe in yourself and your ability. If you make a bad play, you have to forget it and go on to the next job. It took me years to learn to do this, but it is what makes a pro."

How did he train his mind to concentrate?

"I have a regimen to accomplish this. I believe the body controls the mind. Every day after practice I work out. I run a lot and do sit-ups, push-ups and other exercises. I've learned to work as hard as I can. I work until the effort is physically painful. It hurts to keep using the muscles. But I force myself to go on working until I pass through the pain period into a pain-free state. If I keep on working as hard as I can, I enter a second and worse pain period. Then I know it's time to quit.

"By doing this I make the body control the mind. Say it's late in the game and I'm tired. I'm running down the field full speed on the kickoff team and somebody lays a real hard block into me. I'm lying there on the ground. I feel as though I've been broken in half. My mind says I couldn't possibly get up. But my body knows better. It's used to pain from my workouts. So I get on my feet and head for the huddle. If you work hard enough, you can make the body control the mind."

And then he said:

"No one knows what he can really do. We all put a limit on our activities. We are our own worst enemies. If we really work, really drive ourselves to our utter limits, we accomplish things we never thought possible."

I stand in awe of Vince Promuto. A simple man from humble origins, he had marched into the world with no built-in advantages, no special talents, indeed, no idea of life beyond a street-corner brawl. Yet before he was 20, he had discovered a great principle of life. And he learned it not from books, not from others, but from his own effort and experience. *"If we really drive ourselves, we accomplish things we never thought possible."*

Vince Promuto had a right to believe that.

DANIEL F. REEVES

Daniel F. Reeves

> *"He is the most competitive person I've ever known. He's only concerned with one thing and that's to win—no matter what he's doing."*

DAN REEVES is about five-feet-eight and so slight of build he weighs only about 140 pounds. He has lived more than half a century, his hair is graying, his face stamped with wrinkles. The only sport he plays is golf, and he's a duffer at it. In his whole life he has never once thought of playing any sport as a professional. But Reeves is certainly part of the world of professional athletics. As principal owner of the Los Angeles Rams, he has devoted his adult life to pro football, and he has had a great deal to do with the game's present popularity. Without playing himself, he has made it possible for many others to play and for millions to watch them. His election in 1967 to the Football Hall of Fame in Canton, Ohio, placed him in the company of the game's all-time greats.

I wanted to talk to the owner of a professional football team, and I felt that Dan Reeves was the perfect choice. Three years previously, in 1964, I had interviewed Reeves while in Los Angeles on a magazine assignment. He had been most kind to me while I was away from home and had talked to me at great length.

Dan Reeves is a quiet man. He is soft-spoken, shy, reserved, rather somber. He is a formal man. An innate courtesy shadows all his actions, and a person spending any time with him discovers that thoughtfulness, more than simple politeness, is behind his manner. Yet it is important to understand that despite his diminutive appearance and gentle demeanor, Dan Reeves is a very tough individual. As one of his close friends said, "He is the most competitive person I've ever known. He only knows one thing and that's to win – no matter what he's doing."

His quiet but ferocious competitiveness is fueled by a mind that has two primary qualities. First, it is a sponge. He sops up information from every conceivable source. Then he analyzes. He often goes to a blackboard and draws a line down the middle. On one side he marks a plus, on the other a minus. Then he tallies all the facts he has, the pros and cons of an issue, as pluses or minuses on the blackboard. The decision to be made usually reveals itself on the blackboard. The second quality of his mind is single-mindedness. Once the decision has been reached, he pursues it with dedication and monumental thoroughness. He is a perfectionist about details. Choosing new jerseys for the Rams, he sent his staff to a television studio to have the uniforms photographed because he wanted to be certain how they'd look on the screen — in both black and white and color.

Dan Reeves was born in New York, where his father, from a modest beginning, put together a giant chain of more than one thousand grocery stores. Dan grew up in a Fifth Avenue apartment, but not as a spoiled rich man's son. His father believed that hard work was a good teacher and required his sons to work in the stores every day, stacking cans, sweeping the floor, waiting on customers.

Dan Reeves was born rich, yet he has an unusual attitude toward money. One of his close friends says that he almost seems to feel guilty about having wealth. He lives comfortably in a large home formerly owned by actor Basil Rathbone in the posh Bel Air section of Los Angeles. There are three servants who have been in the Reeves family for many years. Yet he does not live ostentatiously. He dresses conservatively. He and his wife are the antithesis of "high society" or the "jet set." In fact, as one friend put it, "Dan's idea of luxury is to drive a Buick."

I have no idea exactly how much money Reeves has, but my impression is that, as millionaires go, he is a modest one. He is not interested in simply accumulating money. His experience as a stockbroker illustrates the point. After his father's stores were sold in 1940, he used his share to buy a seat on the New York Stock Exchange for $60,000. He had no great interest in the stockbrokerage business. He made the move as an investment that would take care of his family in the years ahead. When

Reeves moved to Los Angeles, he opened a stockbrokerage office there. The business grew rapidly until it had three offices employing over 100 account executives buying and selling securities for thousands of customers. Suddenly, Reeves cut it back to one small office employing only three account executives. He was fearful that a recommendation by one of his men might cause a person to lose money, and particularly concerned that his firm, by collecting fees for stock sales, might make money on a customer's misfortune. Reeves's attitude toward money and his unwillingness to accumulate a large fortune have their significance in the Los Angeles Rams' story.

If Dan Reeves had only a passing interest in the stockbrokerage business, he had a passion for football. Despite his size, he had played a little in high school and had always loved the sport. His older brother, Edward, had a small interest in the Washington Redskins in the 1930s, and this sharpened Reeves's appetite to own a professional football team. In 1940, he went shopping for a team and bought the only one up for sale, the Cleveland Rams. The price was $100,000. Reeves bought two-thirds of it and the remainder was purchased by his old college friend, Fred Levy, Jr. Levy was from Louisville, Kentucky, where his family had a fortune founded in department stores and real estate.

Now Reeves owned a football team but not a very good one. Moreover he didn't like Cleveland and couldn't bring himself to move there and take charge of the team. He appointed Billy Evans general manager and remained in New York, though he made frequent visits to Cleveland. These were halted by World War II, when Reeves joined the Air Corps as a second lieutenant.

As a business, the Cleveland Rams were a financial disaster. In 1940, the club lost about $40,000. By 1945 the losses had climbed to $64,000. Reeves had bought out Levy's share and was absorbing all of this himself. What particularly disappointed him was that he presented the Cleveland fans with an excellent football team sparked by a young quarterback named Bob Waterfield, won the NFL championship in 1945 – and still he lost $64,000.

Reeves decided to move the team out of Cleveland. His choice was Los Angeles, which at that time had only a minor league baseball team. But Reeves believed, prophetically, that a great post-war exodus to California would take place. West Coast residents would need spectator sports. Los Angeles could well become a mecca for professional football.

The other league owners, who had to approve the transfer, were not impressed with Reeves's predictions. They could only see the higher travel expenses in transporting their own teams to the West Coast to play the Rams. The owners agreed to the transfer, but only after insisting on favorable terms. Reeves would have to guarantee each opponent $15,000, instead of the $10,000 required of every other league team.

California in 1946 was no promised land for Reeves and the Rams. Attendance lagged and Reeves doubled his Cleveland losses – to $128,000. He explained the reasons for the poor showing in characteristically simple terms. "It was a new sport in a new town and we had stiff competition." The chief problem was that Los Angeles loved football, but college football, namely the Trojans of Southern California and the UCLA Bruins. The rivalry between the two schools was a hot one and their games were pageants of color and excitement. Pro football had a difficult time establishing a following. Another difficulty was the All-American Conference, a rival pro league. The Los Angeles Dons in that league were in direct competition with the Rams and outdrew them, in part because the new league included the San Francisco 49ers and capitalized on the rivalry between the two California cities. Finally, the Rams' record, six wins, four losses and a tie, was not outstanding.

The next year, 1947, the Rams had an even worse season, with a 6–6 record, and Reeves's losses continued to mount. It began to look as though his father should have owned a lot more than one thousand grocery stores.

Actually Reeves faced an even greater financial loss. Under U. S. income tax laws, if a businessman loses money in an enterprise, he may subtract his losses from his other sources of income. So Reeves deducted the $64,000 he lost in Cleveland and the large sum he lost in Los Angeles from his earnings in the stockbrokerage business and other investments. This hardly made the losses painless, but it did anesthetize them a little.

By 1947, Reeves was in his third straight year of losses, with no end in sight. Soon he would have to face a second provision of the income tax law. If a businessman loses $50,000 or more a year for five consecutive years, the government thinks he is very foolish to maintain his enterprise. The government says in effect that this is no longer a business but a hobby (rather accurate in

Reeves's case) and requires that the individual pay, in a lump sum, the tax on the total amount he has deducted from other earnings during the past five years.

To reduce the financial strain on his purse, and to prepare for the possibility that his losses would continue for five years, Reeves decided to take in partners. He would not ask his partners to invest any money in the club — just a nominal one dollar to make the partnership legal — but he would ask them to share the losses. If a partner took 10 per cent ownership for one dollar, he would underwrite 10 per cent of the losses. When and if the club began to make money, he would get 10 per cent of the profits.

"As you can imagine," Reeves said, "it wasn't very easy to find someone willing to invest in a business losing the kind of money we were." But, ultimately, Reeves found his partners. First to come in was Reeves's old pal, Fred Levy, Jr. He was joined by Ed Pauley, one of the richest men in America, with a fortune based in oil and his brother Harold Pauley. On November 1, 1947, an agreement was signed in which Levy and the Pauley brothers, in return for an investment of one dollar, agreed to share in both losses and profits. Specifically, Levy owned 20 per cent of the club, Ed Pauley 27.5 per cent and Harold Pauley 10 per cent. That left Reeves with 42.5 per cent.

In effect, Reeves had given away a controlling interest in his own football team. I asked why. "It was getting to be too much for me financially," he said. "I've always been rather conservative about money. I had funds set aside for my family, and I couldn't touch these. I couldn't expect my family to suffer because of my interest in football. As it was, I just couldn't take these losses much longer. I was extremely grateful to my partners for joining in what was certainly a very bad investment. Besides, I didn't feel I was losing control of the club. The agreement stated that I was to have full authority as general manager. If at any time the other partners objected to the way I was running the club, they could on November 1 of any year exercise their majority rule and remove me. But I never thought any such thing would happen. The Pauleys weren't football men and didn't pretend to be. Besides, Levy was my closest friend. He and I together owned a controlling interest."

The losses kept piling up. In 1947, the first year of the agreement, Reeves share of the losses came to $71,000, Ed Pauley's to $61,000, Harold Pauley's to $22,000, Fred Levy's to $30,000. In 1948, when the Rams had a 6–5–1 season, Reeves lost $104,000, Ed Pauley $67,000, Harold Pauley $24,000 and Fred Levy $49,000.

In 1949, the Rams again lost an aggregate $136,000, although the team won the Western Division title with an 8–2–2 record. Under the agreement Ed Pauley absorbed $37,000 of the loss, Harold Pauley $14,000 and Fred Levy $27,000. That left Reeves to pay $58,000, and, as he put it, "I was getting caught." It would be his fifth consecutive year of losses exceeding $50,000. His business would become a hobby. He would have to pay the whole five years of taxes, about a quarter of a million dollars.

The only way to avoid payment was to take in another partner, and so J. Hal Seley became, for one dollar, an owner of 12.5 per cent of the Los Angeles Rams, accepting in his first year a loss of $22,000. This made Reeves's personal loss "only" $36,000 and saved him from the larger five-year tax loss. Though Reeves saved a quarter of a million dollars, his share in his club shrank to 30 per cent. "But I wasn't worried. Fred Levy and I together owned 50 per cent."

The next year the Rams' fortune turned. The All-American Conference was absorbed into the NFL. The Los Angeles Dons folded, and the Rams were the only team in the area. San Francisco was admitted to the NFL, which set up the Rams-49ers' rivalry. Even better, the Rams had a good football team. Its 9–3 record tied the Chicago Bears for the Western Division title, and the Rams won the play-off game. The title game with the Cleveland Browns was a classic which the Browns won 30–28 on a last minute field goal by Lou (The Toe) Groza. Reeves and his partners broke even that year for the first time.

In 1951, the Rams again won the Western Division title with an 8–4 record and became World Champions. In 1952, the team's 9–3 record tied them with Detriot, which won the playoff. For four consecutive years, the Rams had either won or tied for divisional honors and they had won one world championship. With this record, the Rams attracted a great following. Southern California went pro football crazy, and the huge Los Angeles Coliseum drew crowds never before seen in the sport. In 1952, the Rams played before 944,744 people in 20 exhibition and regular season games, an average of nearly 50,000 per game. An exhibition game against Washington drew 95,985 fans in 1951. But even this would be surpassed. Three times in 1957 and 1958, the Rams drew over 100,000 fans, topped by the 102,368 who witnessed the Rams-49ers game in 1957 – the biggest crowd ever to attend a professional football game. The Rams' seasonal attendance climbed, 1,051,000 in 1957; 1,053,000 in 1958; 1,061,000 in 1959, another league record. The Rams were drawing more fans to an 18-game schedule than most major league baseball teams drew in 154 games.

Reeves and his partners turned the financial corner with a vengeance. Years of losses were superseded by immense profits. I do not know the exact profit figures, but Reeves told me that in return for the $353,000 in losses sustained by the four partners (all of that deducted from other earnings in paying income taxes), the partners received profits of over $2 million during the next 12 years. "I didn't mind," said Reeves. "I most certainly needed them when times were bad. I had no objection to sharing the wealth with them."

It would appear that Reeves's four partners were in a rather ideal situation. Having had the astuteness to gamble on a losing proposition, they had won a fortune. It cannot be said they had invested $353,000 in the Rams. This sum was a tax loss on their other earnings. They had invested one dollar apiece and taken out large profits.

Yet all was not well. The five partners began to quarrel – sometimes violently. All were wealthy, successful, willful and stubborn men, accustomed to having their own way. But the main cause of the quarreling probably was envy.

Reeves said, "It got to be Dan Reeves's Rams in the newspapers and on television. I was always listed as general manager and owner and the other guys not at all. I was interviewed as the source of information. You see, I was active in all trades, signings and player drafts. I never particularly wanted it, but I got to be a celebrity. Everyone knew Dan Reeves. I think this annoyed my partners."

Undoubtedly it did. There is a glamour attached to owning a professional team. Ed Pauley, who had bought his brother's share and owned 37.5 per cent of the club, compared to Reeves's 30 per cent, had little to say about running the team. "Ed would say I ought to do such and such," Reeves admitted. "I'd agree with him but never do anything about it. Sometimes I tried to involve the partners in the club's operation. I asked them to participate in the search for a coach to succeed Harry Gilmer, but nothing ever came of it. The trouble was they all wanted to make the decisions, but they were unwilling to give the time to learn the business. It was a bad situation, yet I can't blame them. If the situation had been reversed, Dan Reeves would have acted as they did."

Reeves's independence of Pauley and Seley undoubtedly stemmed from his belief that he and Levy could control the club. They were, after all, close friends. Levy had moved to Los Angeles and he and Reeves saw each other daily. Their families had been close for more than 20 years. Ed Pauley could become angry, but as long as Levy was on his side, Reeves could not lose control of his club.

Then, on November 1, 1955, Reeves was invited to a meeting of the partners at the plush Beverly Hills Hotel. "I had an inkling right away that something was up. Just the date, the anniversary of the original agreement eight years before, indicated something was going on. The meeting was to be a luncheon in a private room. I walked in and knew right away it was trouble. Ed handed me a sealed letter. I opened it. Under the terms of the agreement, it said, the majority owners wished to appoint the general manager. The majority owners? I looked at my old friend Levy. He said, and I'll never forget it, 'Dan, please tell Ed I didn't let you know about it.' He hadn't, that was for sure. I said one word, 'no,' and walked out of the room."

The result was chaos. Fred Levy had sided with Pauley and Seley to form a majority that wanted Reeves out as general manager. But Reeves still considered the Rams to be his ball club. He wasn't about to step out. It was open war. A lifelong friendship was smashed, and powerful men were at odds.

The next few years provided strong evidence that football games may be won on the gridiron, but the unity and good sense of the front office is instrumental in the process. The Rams had won the divisional title in 1955 with an 8–3–1 record. In 1956, the team had a 6–6 record; in 1958, they were in the thick of the race with an 8–4 record, losing to the Colts; in 1959, they fell to the cellar with a disastrous 2–10 season; they were 4–7–1 in 1960; 4–10 in 1961; an unbelieveable 1–12–1 in 1962.

Attendance climbed for the first few years after the partners fought, then dropped from 1,061,000 in 1959 to 820,000 in 1962.

The other NFL owners realized that the Rams' popularity had helped the whole league to prosper. They knew the squabble among the Rams' owners could damage every other club. So the late Bert Bell, who was then NFL commissioner, was dispatched to effect a compromise among the Rams' owners. Under the terms he worked out, Reeves agreed to step out as general manager in favor of Pete Rozelle (who later succeeded Bell as commissioner). Reeves and the opposing faction each held 50 per cent of the vote and, in the event of a stalemate, the commissioner would make the final decision.

But the compromise didn't work. With Reeves out, Rozelle and Elroy Hirsch, who succeeded him as general manager, were hamstrung by the divided owners. Any coach or player who became dissatisfied could find one of the owners to back him. The team degenerated into factions which squabbled as the owners did. And Reeves was missed. His forte had been scouting and player personnel. With his guiding hand gone, some disastrous trades were made and the Rams failed to take advantage of the player draft.

The situation went on for seven years, a bitter time for Reeves. He had owned and run the Rams in Cleveland and Los Angeles for 15 years, only to see his partners take control. "I was hurt and mad," Reeves said. "I'd thought my friendship with Levy meant more than it apparently did."

For the next few years, Reeves stayed away from his club. "I became involved in three dimensional photography and I bought a half interest in the Los Angeles Blades hockey team. But, honestly, my whole life had been football and I was rather lost."

Reeves began a campaign to win back control of his club. He knew just how difficult the fight would be. He was up against a tough individual in Ed Pauley. (Levy had sold half his 20 per cent to comedian Bob Hope, but Hope had no vote and did not participate in running the club.) Pauley largely dominated Levy and Seley as far as the Rams were concerned. In Pauley, Reeves was facing an aggressive, tough-minded and highly competitive man who was, in addition, perhaps a hundred times wealthier.

Some futile efforts were made to settle the ownership issue in the courts, but by 1959 it had become obvious that either Reeves would buy out Pauley and the others — or vice versa. Reeves agreed to this arrangement in principle, then launched a campaign to make himself buyer.

He applied all his thoroughness and stubbornness to the task. For over two years he did little except wrestle with the problem of buying back his ballclub. The problem was simple mathematics. To buy him out, Pauley, Levy, Seley and Hope had only to purchase 30 per cent of the club. Reeves had to buy 70 per cent — and Reeves simply did not have that much money.

His first step was to find men to back him. Over a period of time, he formed a group headed by former cowboy star Gene Autry. The dozen or so wealthy men in the group agreed to supply money in the unlikely event that Reeves regained control of the club. If the new ownership ever came into existence, Reeves was determined to maintain majority control and to form a corporation, rather than operate the franchise as a partnership. This, he felt, would make the management much more businesslike. Reeves said of this group, "Autry had never before been willing to join a venture which he did not control. I was complimented that he was willing to join this one under my leadership."

Even with this backing, Reeves knew he had scant hope of buying the club. Because of the 70–30 split, Pauley and the others had to put up such a relatively small amount of money that they could beat any price Reeves offered. "The only chance I had was to try to arrange the most favorable terms of sale I could," Reeves said, and his whole effort went into this. No detail of the sale (or, possibly, the purchase) was too small for him to deal with.

A major issue was the nature of the sale. Pauley and the others wanted an auction: the club would be put on the block and the partners would bid orally. The highest bidder would take full title and buy out the others. Reeves was dead set against this. He lacked the capital and knew he would lose. He insisted instead on a sealed bid: both ownership factions would make a sealed offer for the club and the highest bidder would win. Reeves wanted just one bid, but the Pauley faction insisted on subsequent bids. There were prolonged negotiations over this question, but neither side would give ground.

But the more Reeves thought about it, the more he became convinced that subsequent bids might provide a means of victory for him. If the terms of the bidding were just right, he might, *just might* be successful.

So he began to develop a strategy that would make the terms "just right." His first step was to agree to subsequent bids – *under certain conditions.* The first condition was that each subsequent bid had to be significantly higher than the previous best bid. He wanted to avoid the situation in which the highest first bid would be bested by a second bid that was only one dollar higher. This would turn the sale into an auction, which he could not win, since his opponents had the money to out-bid him. Prolonged discussions took place, but finally both sides agreed that all subsequent bids had to be at least 20 per cent higher than the previous high bid.

The second condition Reeves sought was a limited time in which either side could make a subsequent bid. "Negotiations almost broke down on this issue," Reeves said. "They wanted three hours to make another bid. I wanted five minutes. I didn't want to give them a lot of time to think everything over. I wanted to force a quick decision. You see, I knew the others were starting to fight among themselves. I wanted to allow them as little time as possible to agree on a bid. There was a great deal of discussion over the time limit, but finally we compromised on a half-hour to make a new bid."

A half-hour to make a 20 per cent higher bid was the crux of Reeves's plan, but there were dozens of other details that consumed his attention. He wanted the terms of sale and the form of the bids stated in precise legal language so the loser could not have the sale invalidated in the courts. He wanted the sale conducted by Pete Rozelle, the NFL commissioner, and his staff, and he wanted the bids to be opened in public so the press would be present. It would be an advantage, he felt, if the sale were conducted in the proverbial goldfish bowl, so that the terms arrived at could not be subject to argument.

Reeves's planning was so thorough he even insisted that the bids be opened at 10:00 A.M. on December 27, 1962. "I knew," said Reeves, "that my partners would be celebrating a good bit over the Christmas holidays and might not be in their best shape that early in the morning."

All these preparations were designed to make Reeves's bid successful. "I decided very early that I would make only one bid and win or lose with it. I wanted it to be as high as I could possibly make it. I spent a great deal of time trying to figure what to bid. In the end, I took the highest estimate of the real worth of the club — and doubled it. In truth, this figure was every dollar I could possibly scrape up without depriving my family."

On December 27, the sports world of Los Angeles riveted its attention on this strange "battle of the bucks" between the divided owners. Sportswriters compared the procedure to a multi-million dollar poker hand.

It was a dramatic moment as the participants gathered in Suite 126 of the Bel Air Hotel. A tense Pete Rozelle was there, and Elroy Hirsch, the Rams' general manager, looking as though he'd break into pieces if anyone touched him. Other Rams' employees were in no better shape. Pauley, Levy and Seley seemed confident: they were odds-on favorites to win. They and everyone else knew simple arithmetic was on their side. Since they had only to buy Reeves's 30 per cent share, they could afford to pay an extremely high price.

Outwardly Reeves was reasonably successful in masking his feelings, but he was entirely pessimistic, so much so that he carried a prepared statement conceding defeat: "I shall always be grateful to the many people who have been so generous to the Rams and to me. To the Rams I wish good luck and to Mr. Pauley and his group I extend goodwill." He felt he had no chance of winning.

The room, crowded with news reporters and photographers, became quiet as Rozelle prepared to open the sealed bids. Pauley and his group bid $6,100,000. This was extremely high and Reeves was surprised. The bid was at least a million dollars more than he had anticipated. The $6,100,000 figure meant that Pauley and his group would pay Reeves over $1,800,000 for his 30 per cent share. The sum was amazing. In 1957 Reeves had offered to sell his share to Pauley for $2,000,000. Pauley had refused, stating the price was exorbitant. Now he was offering almost as much. He really wanted the ballclub. And Reeves knew he would have it with his subsequent bid.

Reeves's bid was opened to reveal a fantastic figure of $7,100,000, the highest price ever offered for any sports franchise. This meant he would have to pay the other owners almost $5,000,000 to buy back what they had paid one dollar apiece for. Suite 126 rang with noise as the bid was announced.

Reeves's bid meant that the next bid, at a minimum of 20 per cent higher, would have to be more than $8,500,-000. Would Pauley, Levy and Seley pay it? They had a half-hour to decide, and they retired to another suite down the hall to deliberate.

Reeves was certain they would pay the price. Even at this high figure, the other owners would need to pay Reeves a little over $2,500,000. There was no doubt they could afford it and, knowing Pauley's competitive spirit, Reeves felt doomed. Well, at least he would have gotten a top price for his holdings.

Suite 126 buzzed in anticipation. The minutes dragged slowly until it seemed Pauley, Levy and Seley were out of the room for hours. Actually, only 15 minutes elapsed before they reappeared. Silence descended on the room as Pauley pulled a piece of paper from his pocket and began to read:

"We congratulate Daniel Reeves on his successful bid at the auction which took place today under the jurisdiction of Pete Rozelle. We wish him great success in his conduct of the Rams football team and will remain loyal fans and supporters of the team."

There would be no subsequent bid. Reeves had bought back his own team.

Suite 126 erupted. It was bedlam, with everyone laughing and crying and shrieking, some all at the same time. Elroy Hirsch, who as "Crazy Legs Hirsch" had been one of the toughest NFL running backs, burst into tears. His eyes were still red at a hastily called press conference a few minutes later. Happily demoted from general manager to assistant, he said, "I want to stay as long as Dan wants me." Reeves said of his former partners, "I had always considered them to be as crazy as I was. The price is too high when you consider the earnings, but then I value money lower than some people."

An unanswered question even today is why Pauley and the others did not make the subsequent bid of $8,500,000. Reeves believes that "the price was too high. My bid of $7,100,000 was ridiculous. To have paid almost one and a half million more would have made them look foolish. I feel that as much as Pauley hated to lose, he hated to look like a business fool the more." This view was supported by a spokesman for Pauley who said, "Ed felt he couldn't in all conscience" raise the offer. As a business investment the club was worth his original $6,100,000 bid and no more.

There were other reasons. Pauley, Levy, Seley and to a lesser extent Hope were being roasted in the press. Jim Murray of the *Los Angeles Times* put the matter bluntly: "In 1955, Pauley organized the dollar-a-year club members and demanded a more active voice in the management. Reeves reacted as if they were just people he had invited to dinner who began to demand he fire the cook, change the wallpaper in their bedrooms and then asked him to move out into the guest house. . . . It's just possible Ed Pauley figured, with the rest of the populace, he had stayed to dinner too long and bade his host good night with a handshake and, at last, a gesture of gallantry."

There was more substance than gallantry in the transaction. For their original one dollar apiece, the partners had obtained a useful $353,000 tax loss and profits estimated at $2,000,000, then sold their shares back to Reeves – Pauley for $2,200,000, Levy for $1,600,000 (half of which went to Hope) and Seley for $1,020,000. It had been one of the better investments any man ever made.

Reeves had reacquired a club with a 1–12–1 record in 1962. As general manager, he began to rebuild the Rams. It was a slow process in a league that included such powerhouse teams as Green Bay, Dallas, Baltimore and Cleveland. His specialty had always been scouting and player selection, but his magic was hampered by the expansion of the NFL to Minnesota, Atlanta and New Orleans, and competition from the American Football League. The talented college players were in great demand. Still, the Rams began to show steady improvement, and in 1967, they were second to Green Bay in the NFL's Western Division.

Reeves has definite ideas about scouting. "When I came into the league," he says, "scouting consisted of reading the papers and calling up a few college coaches and ex-players to ask them to cover a prospect or recommend one. It was all much too hit or miss. I felt it had to be systematized. After all, the player draft afforded a team the chance to rebuild, if the right players were drafted."

But who were the right players? Reeves began hiring full-time scouts on his payroll. They compiled dossiers on each likely man in every college, large or small.

"You have no idea how difficult it is to gain information. If we could learn the height, weight and time speed of every prospect, that would be 40 per cent of the battle. It would be ideal if we could walk into a dressing room, measure and weigh a man and then take him out on the field with a stop watch. But no coach will allow that, so we have to depend upon information that is often sketchy. Many coaches, wanting their men to make good, have a tendency to exaggerate their capabilities. The programs printed for games are often downright lies. We signed a prospect who was listed as six-feet-four in the program. In training camp he turned out to be only six-feet-one. An amazing number of boys 'lose' 25 to 40 pounds between college and reporting to training camp.

"Take speed. The coach says, 'Oh, yes he's fast, all right. He does the 40 in 4.7.' It isn't that the coach is lying, but what are the conditions? Was he wearing track clothes or a full football uniform? Was there a tail wind to help him? How fast does he truly run? We often don't know till we get him to camp and time him.

"There are other factors. Is his frame such that he will put on weight? A boy may weigh only 175 pounds, but with a program of isometrics and weight lifting he could put on 40 pounds, if he has the frame to take it.

"But the great intangible is mental attitude. Is he intelligent? Does he have a quick mind to learn plays, yet a retentive memory? Does he have desire? Does he want to play so badly he'll work as hard as is necessary? Does he like body contact? Will he become discouraged under adversity? Can he control his temper and use it effectively? Has he the capacity to improve or has he already reached his peak? There are scores of factors to be considered. I wish we had a psychological test that would answer some of these questions in advance. We too often don't get the answers until long after a player has been in competition."

In the past Reeves built the Rams by scouting and signing the best prospects. His system didn't always work. One choice Reeves would like to make over was the selection of Jim Arnett of UCLA instead of Jimmy Brown of Syracuse. Arnett was a good runner, but Brown became the greatest the game has ever known. But if mistakes were made, there were also many successes. "We'd have perhaps 42 players in camp, all of them capable of playing in the league, and our roster was limited to 32. So we'd trade off the rest for draft choices." Sometimes this process leads to mistakes. Reeves's scouts correctly appraised the worth of John Unitas. He was signed, then traded. "I wish we had that one to do over," Reeves laments.

In recent years, since the expansion of pro football, Reeves has been making more trades for proven players and relying less on the draft, though he has not abandoned it.

Reeves still spends most of his waking hours immersed

in football, either with the Rams or in league activities. He was a prime mover in the merger between the American and National Football Leagues. Football keeps him busy and being busy with football he acts like the happiest man in the world, which he just might be.

BOB FELLER

JP

Bob Feller

"I grew up absolutely certain, not just that I would be a major league pitcher, but the greatest who ever lived."

Bob Feller is nine years older than I am. When he was a rookie with the Cleveland Indians, I was a nine-year-old growing up in Ohio. I was a passionate fan. I followed his entire career and saw him pitch many times. He was my boyhood idol. Thirty years and more later, I must admit I felt some anticipation as I turned into the entrance of his estate to meet him for the first time.

"Estate" is the word. I drove through a massive stone gate and drove along a quarter mile of winding road through what could qualify as a public park. Ultimately, I reached an immense three-story stone "castle" fronted by an oval courtyard large enough to park the fleet of a sizable car rental agency, with a couple of buses thrown in. A brace of hound dogs greeted me, and I felt like I was entering the set of an old movie starring Ronald Coleman as an aristocratic English gentleman.

I was greeted by Feller's second son, Martin, a junior at Brown University. He explained that his father would be late. Would I mind waiting? I was ushered into a small but ornate study decorated in various shades of gilt, served a ginger ale and offered magazines and the Cleveland newspapers. Mrs. Feller appeared and greeted me warmly. She was a very tiny woman. She wore a vintage sweater and appeared to be doing housework. Her casualness made me feel at home.

I waited for Feller for two hours. During most of this time Martin kept me company. We talked about baseball and his father's career. A lot of our talk centered on statistics. This was not strange. One of the peculiarities of baseball is its devotion to statistics. Sportscasters, for example, employ corps of statisticians so that they can announce new records the moment old ones are broken. The 1967 World Series was an inning and a half old when, as the announcer pointed out, a World Series record was tied. Dalton Jones, the Red Sox third baseman, had started a double play in two consecutive innings.

I suspect that sportscasters imposed statistics on baseball. The game is a slow-moving one. The pitcher may stand on the mound for 30 or 40 seconds before delivering a pitch. Two or three minutes may elapse between half innings. The announcer fills the time by reporting statistics. Mickey Mantle is batting such and such left-handed and something else right-handed. If time permits, the announcer may present a breakdown of the switch-hitting Mantle's home runs, triples, doubles, total bases and walks for each side of the plate.

Baseball statistics become absurd sometimes, yet they are part of the game. I've often wondered what a player really thinks when his records are broken.

He usually says something like: "Records are made to be broken. I'm glad such a fine athlete broke mine." I've doubted that statements like that are sincere.

I wanted to talk to Bob Feller, the great pitching star of the Cleveland Indians, because he was one of the great pitchers of all time. He set records that promised to last for decades: most strike-outs in a nine-inning game (18); most strike-outs in a season (348); most no-hitters in a lifetime (3); most one-hitters in a lifetime (12) – among many others. He was elected to the Hall of Fame the moment he became eligible.

I knew that Feller's records had not lasted. A pitcher named Sandy Koufax broke most of them. He struck out 19 in a game, 382 in a season, and pitched four no-hitters, one of them a perfect game.

I wanted to ask Feller about this. How did it feel to see your name superseded in the record books by another man's? Feller agreed to the interview readily, but arranging it took time, Feller has varied business interests in insurance, real estate, securities, military food supplies and baseball. He travels a great deal. Finally, I pinned down the appointment, at his home in Gates Mills, a Cleveland suburb, in late August.

The Bob Feller who finally appeared was somewhat overwhelming. He had great energy. He spent most of the interview pacing the floor of the small room, rubbing his hands together or gesturing broadly. This was not out of impatience with my questions. Rather, he enjoyed the interview. Only his wife's announcement that dinner was served stopped our talk. Even then we stood outside in the courtyard talking for another 15 minutes. Besides his energy, Feller impressed me with his enthusiasm and his personal magnetism. Even his voice was awesome. It was extremely low, a sort of guttural growl. When he answered the phone, he said, "Fellers," with a sound resembling a wounded grizzly bear trapped in his lair. He reminded me of Unitas. They shared that quality of positiveness and let's-get-on-with-the-job self-confidence.

Feller did not go with his house. The estate led to an expectation of Tudor aristocracy and polished manners. Feller was born an Iowa farmboy and he was still as honest and direct as the dirt he used to plow. He was much, much too direct to be polished. He was rough, homespun, extremely informal. I was sure the brown sports jacket and gray trousers he wore were expensive, yet I felt he was too uninterested in clothes to wear them well. He looks much as he did in his playing days, brown hair slicked straight back and parted on the side, big brown eyes, generous lips that roll back in a smile to present a strong set of teeth. His weight could not be five pounds greater than it was in his prime.

We had a far-ranging conversation about baseball. Feller had a quick mind, and he tended to move quickly from idea to idea, yet in the end I was happy with the result.

We talked about records. I don't think there is any doubt that Feller's records meant a great deal to him.

He did not bemoan the fact that Koufax broke them. He was too mature, too wealthy, too successful in business to build his life around anything as flimsy as a statistic. Nor did he care that the records were of such short duration. It was setting them that meant so much to him.

When Bob Feller was a boy in Van Meter, Iowa, he threw the ball so hard he was a freak. It is an unprovable statement, for no records are kept of the speed of a thrown ball, but Feller probably threw harder than anyone who ever played baseball.

"When I was in the fourth or fifth grade," Feller said, "I could throw the ball harder and farther than high school kids. My father used to catch me using a feather pillow. I never thought about anything but baseball, and I had no idea I wouldn't succeed. I wasn't the least bit surprised when I did. When I was young, the only question was the position I would play. I was a good infielder. In my early teens I played shortstop and second base on American Legion teams, and I could hit in those days. Later on I found – rather the pitchers discovered – I couldn't hit the curve ball, but back in Iowa I had a difficult time choosing the position best for me.

"When I was 15, I decided to be a pitcher and led our team to the American Legion championship. When I was 16, we lost the championship by a 1–0 score. That year I averaged 19.6 strike-outs a game against the best players in Iowa. I was a local phenom, receiving lots of writeups in the *Des Moines Register and Tribune.* As an amateur I pitched for semi-pro teams. We'd tour the state playing for $100 a game and a tank of gas. Of course I changed my name in each town we visited."

I asked Feller how he could throw so hard. One of my most memorable moments as an interviewer then ensued: Bob Feller in the study of his home, demonstrating that unforgettable pitching form I'd seen so many times from the stands. He made that big windup and reared back on his right leg so far that his left leg was almost vertical to the floor. Then he propelled himself forward across the study floor. All the while, he maintained a running description.

"I'd put my whole body into a pitch, my shoulder, chest and back. Then I'd bring the arm forward with the elbow bent back as far as I could and, at the right moment, I'd bring the last two feet of forearm down, like I was cracking a bullwhip."

Over and over Feller showed me his delivery. He wanted me to understand how he cracked the bullwhip to get the speed, and, to my delight, with each motion, even though he was just practicing in his study, his face bore the same famous grimace it had during 20 years on the mound, as he twisted his lips and exposed his teeth over his lower lip. Apparently, he couldn't deliver a pitch without also delivering that famous scowl.

"When I was young, I used to practice my delivery by the hour. I'd practice leaning way back on my foot —" and he showed how he did that "— so I could keep my balance. I'd have no ball in my hand and I wouldn't attempt to throw. I just practiced keeping my balance. Then, I'd work on my stride. We had a room with a low ceiling. I'd work out in there, and I'd know I was pitching right when my hand just touched the ceiling." Feller couldn't reach the ceiling of his study, but standing there, going through the motions of long ago, I'm sure he was once again touching the farmhouse ceiling.

"Like I say, I grew up absolutely certain, not just that I would be a major league pitcher, but the greatest who ever lived. I started to follow big league ball in 1928 and by 1929 I was all wrapped up in it. I used to follow Walter Johnson a lot, but, like everyone else in Iowa, I was a St. Louis Cardinal fan. I watched Dizzy Dean pitch against Detroit in the 1934 World Series. My father took me to Sportsman's Park in St. Louis. That was the first major league game I ever saw.

"When the majors became interested in me, it was a tossup between Cleveland and the Cardinals. My father didn't much like the Cardinal organization, so I went with Cleveland. I signed with scout Cy Slapnicka while sitting on a tractor in the fields."

Feller was moving into one of the great eras of baseball. Babe Ruth was retiring, but Lou Gehrig was still playing, along with Jimmy Foxx, Hank Greenberg, Charley Gehringer, Mickey Cochrane, Mel Ott, Bill Terry, Joe Medwick, Johnny Mize, Luke Appling, Paul Waner, Carl Hubbell, Paul Derringer, Lefty Grove, Lefty Gomez, Red Ruffing, Schoolboy Rowe and many, many outstanding players. Rookies named Stan Musial, Joe Dimaggio and Ted Williams were coming up, too.

It was a time of great sluggers and .375 batting averages, yet Feller, sitting on the tractor and scrawling his signature, was convinced that he would not just make the majors but become the greatest pitcher of all time, better than Cy Young, Walter Johnson, Grover Alexander, Christy Mathewson. True, perhaps every rookie expects to rewrite the record books, but Feller wasn't dreaming. As he put it, "When I came up I had lots of confidence. I wasn't scared. I was determined, excited, raw, but I had no doubt I would be the greatest pitcher who ever lived."

Such a statement sounds dreadfully conceited. But Feller's performance instantly matched his anticipations. He never played a minute in the minors. Going straight to the majors is not uncommon today, but in 1936, it was unheard of. Even the best prospects spent two to five years in the minors for "seasoning."

Feller first wore a Cleveland uniform in an exhibition game against the St. Louis Cardinals, the famed "Gashouse Gang," on July 6, 1936. He pitched only three innings, but what innings they were! He allowed two hits, walked one — and struck out eight. There is an often-reported story that Leo Durocher, the Cards' colorful shortstop, took two strikes and walked toward the dugout. The umpire supposedly called him to come back, saying he still had another strike. Durocher said, "Why bother?" Feller said this story is apocryphal. More truthful was Dizzy Dean's remark when a photographer asked him to pose with Feller. "It's all right with me, but you'd better ask him if it's okay with him. After what he did today, he's the guy to say."

In his first major league start on August 23, 1936, Feller struck out 15 St. Louis Browns players. It was the first time an American League pitcher had struck out as many as 15 since 1919. Twenty-one days later he fanned 17 Philadelphia Athletics to tie Dizzy Dean's major league record. On October 2, 1938, he struck out

18 Detroit Tigers, setting the record which lasted until Koufax.

Feller was an instant star, the darling of fans and sportswriters who dubbed him "Rapid Robert." His fast ball brought roars from the stands, which were full whenever he pitched. Each appearance led to an expectation of a new record. His fast ball was clocked at over 100 miles an hour, and he was considered the fastest pitcher of all time. Even more devastating, but not nearly so renowned, was his curve ball, which he threw just as hard as his fast ball. But what made him such a terror on the mound was his lack of control. He was wild, walking almost as many men as he struck out. In those days batters wore no helmets, and it was a brave man who dug in against Feller.

Despite his strike-out totals, Feller's victories lagged. He won five that first abbreviated season, but only 9 in 1937. The next year it was 17. Then, starting in 1939, he began to hit his stride, recording seasons of 24–9, 27–11 and 25–13 in the next three years.

By the end of the 1941 season, Feller was unrivaled as the best right-hander in baseball. In a little over five seasons, he had won 107 games and struck out 1,233 batters in 1,449 innings. He was a superstar of galactic proportions. Feller himself said, "I was ahead of the great pitchers of the modern era in almost every category, including wins and strike-outs." Feller's boyhood determination to rewrite the record book seemed easily within his grasp.

Feller's dream was smashed in the thunder and death of World War II. He spent 44 months in the Navy, winning eight battle stars while serving aboard battleships. He spent the 1942, 1943, 1944 and most of the 1945 seasons in the service. These were the prime years of his mid-twenties. The most conservative estimate is that those four seasons cost him 100 victories and 1,000 strike-outs. Without them most records were beyond his reach.

Feller talked about the war years without bitterness. "Everyone went into the service. I wanted to go and would have had it no other way. What did baseball mean at a time like that? And I was lucky. I survived without injury. How many guys paid a much, much higher price than I did?"

The Feller who came back from the service was at the tail end of his prime. He had a few great years. In his first full season, 1946, he won 26 games. He said of this season: "When I came out of the service, all the records I had hoped to break were beyond reach. About the only thing I could go for were a few strike-out records." So he went for the seasonal record, striking out 348 that year, a total not surpassed until Koufax in 1965.

The 1947 season was crucial for Feller. He tore ligaments in his shoulder and was out a month but still managed to win 20 games. In 1948, he got off to a slow start, but won 9 out of 10 in Cleveland's drive toward the pennant. He started two games in the World Series and lost both, the first to Johnny Sain of the Boston (now Atlanta) Braves on a disputed pick-off play at second. Umpire Bill Steward called Phil Masi safe at second but photographs from every angle showed him to be out. Masi scored on a single to make Feller a 1–0 loser.

The next couple of seasons were not good for Feller. In 1949 he was 15–14 and in 1950 16–11. His strike-outs fell to 108 and 119 in those years. He had lost his fast ball.

"In my early years I never learned to pitch, simply because I didn't have to. I didn't develop real good control and walked a lot of men. My trouble was that I didn't concentrate until I had men on base. You see, I always knew that if I got in trouble, I could throw the ball by the batter for a strike-out. If I'd concentrated and bored down all the time, I would have done a lot better. I lost a lot of games foolishly. But by the late forties, I had lost enough of my fast ball so I no longer could throw it by the hitters. I had to learn to be a pitcher, not just a thrower."

It took Feller a couple of seasons to adjust. He developed a slider to go with his fast ball and curve and began to study hitters and pitch to their weaknesses. He had a good year in 1952, winning 22 and losing eight. He pitched his third no-hitter that year. But that was Feller's last great season. He remained with Cleveland for five more seasons, winning 10 games in 1953 and 13 in 1954, but he was a "spot" pitcher.

These statistics are misleading, for actually Feller had become a wise and cagey pitcher. In 1954, for example, he started only 19 games and won 13 of them. Early in 1955, he pitched the last of 12 one-hitters. Feller was used infrequently, because Cleveland had what is often called the greatest pitching staff ever assembled. Bob Lemon, Early Wynn and Mike Garcia were 20-game winners in 1953. The next year, Lemon and Wynn again won 20 while Garcia had 19. The bullpen was headed by young, hard-throwing Ray Narleski and Don Mossi. Feller was the "spot" pitcher on this staff.

Feller was openly critical of the Cleveland manager, Al Lopez, for not starting him more. "The only type of pitcher Lopez was interested in were those who threw the high hard one." Another time he said, "My troubles with Lopez dated back to his playing days. He was a catcher with us and a good one, but I always preferred to be caught by Rollie Hemsley. Lopez knew that and didn't like it or me very much."

Another sore point with Feller was the 1954 World Series. Cleveland soared to a pennant with 111 victories, a major league record. Heavily favored because of its great pitching, Cleveland was devastated by the New York Giants, who won the first three games with circus catches by Willie Mays in center and pinch homers by Dusty Rhodes. Feller was a sentimental favorite to start the fourth game and fulfill his ambition to win a Series game. He had lost in '48 on the disputed play, then been hit hard in his second start. In 1954, Cleveland fans wanted him to be given a chance. Lopez went with Lemon, who lost the fourth game.

I asked Feller about the incident. He spoke of it as a long-ago, half-forgotten episode, remarking that Lopez had to go with Lemon, who was the best on the staff. But earlier, Feller's son Martin had told me that his father had been bitter about not starting a game in the '54 Series.

Feller retired after the 1956 season with a lifetime total of 266 wins and 2,575 strike-outs. As remarkable as these figures are, they pale before the "what might have been." It does not take much speculation to imagine Feller winning 400 games. The war years cost him 100 to 120 wins. More starts during his waning years could have meant another 20 to 25 wins and a lifetime total of about 400. His strike-out total would certainly have exceeded 4,000.

Having set out deliberately to break records and be acknowledged as the greatest pitcher of all time, Feller had been thwarted in this ambition by World War II. But he had come back to become the strike-out king of his day. Then Sandy Koufax moved onto the scene.

I asked Feller what he thought of Koufax.

"I don't really know him personally, but I did enjoy watching him pitch. He didn't throw as hard as I did, and his curve was slower, but he had much better control than I ever did. We were different types of pitchers, and, of course, he was left-handed. I don't know why, but left-handers seem to have an advantage."

Had he been disappointed when his strike-out records were broken?

"No, I always knew they wouldn't last. Actually, I thought Herb Score would be the one to break them. Until he was hurt, he was way ahead of my pace in every category. Koufax never did as well as Score."

Feller continued: "This is the strike-out era. Almost anybody can strike out eight, 10 or 12 batters in a game. Just the other night here Louis Tiant struck out 15 in seven innings. He appeared to have the record well in hand, but unfortunately didn't fan anybody the rest of the game.

"The number of strike-outs today is way up over what it was in my day. There are many reasons for this. The batters are younger and more inexperienced today. Everybody is going for the fences and free swingers are always easier to strike out. It was the little guy who choked up on the bat and just tried to meet the ball who scared me. Night baseball makes it easier for the pitcher. The batter sees only the top half of the ball and can't follow it as well. There's more travel and players sleep in air-conditioned hotel rooms, which I don't think is good for them. Everything is different. The ball is livelier and the bats are lighter and more whiplike. The strike zone is bigger and every pitcher has the slider, which hardly existed when I came up. Nobody tries to pitch complete games anymore. Where a staff had one or two relief pitchers in my time, a staff now has six, seven, eight. Each guy is expected to throw as hard as he can, then be relieved in a couple of innings. The minor leagues are all but gone. When I started, there were 15 guys in the minors for every one in the majors. Now a club is lucky if it has three or four men being readied to move up. Winter baseball was unusual in the 1930's. Now it is commonplace. Players stay in shape the year around.

"Baseball is just not the same game today as 30 years ago. Just look at the batting averages. When I broke in there were maybe two dozen guys in each league batting over .300 and the leaders were always well over .350. Today there are five .300 hitters in each league at the most and .320 wins the batting title.

"Because baseball is so different, I don t see how it's possible to compare Koufax and me, or Roger Maris' 61 home runs in 1961 with Babe Ruth's 60 in 1927. Now there are sports where comparisons can be made. Jim Ryun's record for the mile can certainly be compared with a fellow like Glenn Cunningham who ran in another era. Both wore the same uniform and shoes. The tracks were essentially the same. A swimmer like Don Schollander can be compared to a Johnny Weismuller. The uniform is the same and water is still water. Ryun and Schollander are simply better. They eat better, train harder, have tougher competition. All this is reflected in their improved performance. But can you compare a pole vaulter using a whiplike fiberglass pole with a fellow who used a bamboo pole? I don't think so. The equipment used to set the record is improved."

Feller was quite dynamic now. He paced the floor and gestured broadly. He was entirely wrapped up in what he was saying.

"I don't know if it is original with me, but it seems to me that the only way to compare performances from different baseball eras is to compare a man's performance with the average of his contemporaries. When I was pitching, strike-outs were far less common. Batting averages were higher, more runs were scored and a pitcher would have a good earned-run average if he gave up three runs a game. Now top pitchers will have an earned run average of less than 2. When I was pitching the average number of strike-outs per nine-inning game was less than three. The last time I checked, which was a couple of years ago, the average strike-outs per game was just under six. In other words, the average number of strike-outs has about doubled in a quarter of a century.

"It seems to me the only way to compare Koufax and me is to compare our performances with the average of our contemporaries. I averaged eight strike-outs a game when the league average was about two. Koufax averaged 10 or 12 when the league average was about five or six. In other words, I did a little over three times better than my contemporaries, while Koufax was about twice as effective as his contemporaries. If this measurement was applied to someone like Babe Ruth, the result would be fantastic. Ruth was so far ahead of his contemporaries in hitting home runs that a player might have to hit several hundred homers today to make the same comparison with the average of his contemporaries.

"With the growing number of strike-outs per game, I had no doubt my records would be broken. If anything I was surprised they lasted as long as they did. And Koufax's records will be beaten, too. Strike-outs are here to stay."

I am not a sports statistician, but I made an effort to develop Feller's idea of comparing players' performances with the average of their contemporaries. In 1920, Babe Ruth hit 54 home runs. In that year a total of 370 homers were hit in the American League. The average number of home runs hit by players in the league that year, including Ruth, was about two. But since the roster included pitchers, who are not expected to be sluggers, I felt a fairer comparison was this: among all the players who hit home runs in 1920, the average was four-and-one-half a season. Ruth was a giant compared to the average slugger. In 1966, there were 1,365 home runs hit in the American League. The average performance among those who hit any homers was nine. Applying Feller's method, one could conclude that a player would have to hit about 110 home runs to equal Ruth's 1920 feat.

Feller suggested that if his method was applied to batting averages, it might be found that a .320 average today compared favorably with the .400 hitter of the past. I attempted to do this with an interesting result. In 1920, George Sisler won the American League batting crown with a .407 average. That year the league average was .259. Sisler batted 148 points higher than the average of his contemporaries. In 1966, Frank Robinson won the batting crown with a .316 average, one of the lowest on record. The average of his contemporaries was .240, so Robinson batted 76 points higher. Feller's assumption was wrong. But again the statistics indicated that the old performer was at a higher level above his contemporaries than today's leading player. It is interesting, too, that the league average shrank only 20 points, while the top batter dropped seven times as much. Why would night baseball, travel, new pitches and the other factors cited by Feller have relatively less effect on the average player than on the best? Is the answer that there were giants on the earth in the old days? Perhaps so.

Feller wasn't too impressed with today's baseball. "I'm too busy to go to many games," he said, "and frankly, when I do I find them rather dull. The owners are just interested in filling the stands by having close games and tight pennant races. They couldn't care less about the caliber of play. Everybody knows the minors are dying, if not dead already, but nobody does anything about it and so the whole sport has deteriorated. The games are not much fun to watch. When I go, or watch a game on television, I enjoy seeing a good player, but there aren't too many of those."

I asked him to name a few he enjoyed watching.

"Oh, Koufax when he played, Mantle, this fellow Reichardt with California. Max Alvis with the Indians is a real hustler. I enjoy Brooks Robinson of the Orioles. He's good for baseball. There are undoubtedly others, but I haven't seen enough games and, of course, being in Cleveland I don't know much about the National League."

Did he ever consider returning to baseball as a pitching coach or manager.

"Oh my, no. There isn't enough money in it for one thing. Besides, I'm too independent to take orders from some guy, whether he was the owner or manager, if I didn't think he knew what he was talking about. I'm happy out of baseball. I've always been active in sandlot ball. We have some good teams here, and I work with the boys and pitch batting practice. I attend clinics around the country and try to help the younger fellows. That's much more enjoyable to me than being involved in professional baseball, the way it's played today."

Bob Feller impressed me as a colorful, dynamic man. The air seemed filled with sparks all the time I was with him. His disgust, even bitterness, at today's brand of baseball struck me as a little strange, a little excessive. Then I reflected that old timers often think the youngsters have "gone to pot." And, of course, Feller's criticisms have some validity. That aside, his solidity as a person, his energy and force of personality, provided the dominant image.

Talking to Feller, I was reminded of the time three years previously when I was writing an article about Jim Brown, the great fullback. He was making his first movie and I was trying to determine what kind of an actor he was. In the process, I talked to Richard Boone, the celebrated movie and television actor. He said, "Brown will be a good actor. You see, he's a champion, the greatest runner in the history of football. When a man is a champion at anything, it does things to him. It gives him a dignity, an awareness of self-worth, a self-knowledge and confidence which can never be taken away from him and which the rest of us can only envy." Like Brown, Feller is this kind of man.

STAN MUSIAL

Stan Musial

"I never spent a boring day on the field. I loved to play. I just couldn't wait to get on the field. It was a thrill for me every day."

BUSCH MEMORIAL STADIUM is huge. It seats nearly 50,000 people in two decks covered by a magical roof that needs no columns to support it. Every seat has an unobstructed view. The ball-park is, as sportswriters like to say, "a jewel." In fact, the ridges and delicate arches that decorated its roof reminded me of an immense and beautiful bracelet.

I arrived at the stadium about 6:00 P.M., two hours before game time, picked up my pass and was admitted to the press box. For the next five hours I enjoyed myself immensely. The sky was loaded with stars, and the night was pleasantly warm, "a beautiful night for baseball," as the announcer probably said. The game marked a few firsts for me. It was the first time I had ever sat in a press box. My, those writers have good seats! I was behind home plate, high enough to look down over the whole field, yet close enough to feel almost as if I were part of the play. The press box had comfortable chairs and long steel benches for the writers to work on. There was a lunchroom that turned out an unending stream of sandwiches and beverages without charge. Since I hadn't taken time for dinner, I made a few trips to it, so many, in fact, that I became an old friend to the gracious women dispensing the food.

It was also the first time I had ever arrived at a stadium so early, and I enjoyed watching both the Cardinals and the Dodgers take fielding and batting practice. There was a lot of work, but a lot of fooling around, too. Like little leaguers, the players were letting off steam before the game.

And it was the first National League game I had ever seen. I realized this with surprise when the umpire leaned over the plate, not directly behind the catcher as he does in the American League, but off to one side. I had seen dozens of games, but not until that moment did I realize that every one had been in an American League city. There was a big crowd in the stands: St. Louis already had pennant fever in August. The Redbirds had a 10-game lead and, barring a collapse, they were a shoo-in for the pennant.

Don Drysdale, the great Dodger ace, was on the mound against Larry Jaster, who had a 6–0 record lifetime against Los Angeles. For 10½ innings, scoring consisted of four solo home runs, two by each club. Los Angeles tied the game in the late innings with a pinch homer by Jim Campanis, a substitute catcher. Campanis went behind the plate and, in the last of the eleventh inning, became the goat. The Cardinals loaded the bases with nobody out. The next batter popped a foul behind first which was taken easily by the first baseman. He then threw to Campanis standing in front of the plate. It was a routine play, but Campanis failed to catch the ball. It skidded 10 feet in back of the plate and the Cardinals scored the winning run for a 3–2 victory.

The Cardinals impressed me as an exciting team. They hit, they ran, they were aggressive and confident. "Breaks" seemed to come their way and they made the most of them.

I was glad that I would shortly be talking to their general manager, Stan Musial. From the beginning I'd planned to interview the general manager of a baseball team. I had already talked to Reeves, who was general manager of the Rams as well as an owner. It seemed logical to talk to a man from a different sport. Musial was an obvious choice. By midsummer of 1967, the Cards were in first place, and Musial, as a rookie general manager, was getting a great deal of the credit. In addition, he had, of course, been one of baseball's great players.

To arrange the interview, I called the Cardinals' office in St. Louis, and a day later, Jim Toomey, the director of public relations, called to say Musial would see me in the press box on the day I had selected. Everything Stan Musial touches, I discovered, seems to go smoothly.

Musial was a long time in showing up and even then he just shook hands and said he'd see me later. So it wasn't until nine o'clock or after that we sat down to talk. Meanwhile, I enjoyed the game and the refreshments and chatted with some of the St. Louis sportswriters. They asked the expected questions about who I was and what I was doing there. And I asked them how they accounted for the fact the Cardinals, a sixth-place team the year before, were running away with what was predicted to be a close, six-team race. One fellow said, "Like any pennant winner, several players are having real good years at the same time." I persisted. Was there any reason for that? "Oh," he said ,"it's a happy club. Musial gets a lot of the credit. You know, the happy-go-lucky general manager with a happy-go-lucky team." This, I discovered, was the theme most sportswriters adopted through the remainder of the season.

Musial eventually returned and was waylaid briefly by a couple of sportswriters, so I had a chance to observe him. He wore a bright blue suit with a yellow pinstripe which nearly qualified as Mod, and its effect was to suggest that its wearer was somewhat avant garde. Many sportswriters had written that Musial looked fit enough to go back into uniform. My feeling was that he had put on a little paunch, but he certainly looked healthy. He has brown hair, well trimmed and combed straight back. His eyes are blue and his tanned face has that wrinkled, somewhat leathery look of a man who had spent a lot of time in the sun. In his conversation with the writers, he smiled a great deal. He seemed a relaxed, easygoing fellow, yet I detected some tension in him. He was a bit of a tiger waiting for the cage door to open.

When he came over to me, I formed an instant impression of him, and this was reinforced as I spent more time with him. I decided that Musial had a rare and happy ability to integrate with his surroundings. Whatever he did seemed appropriate to the situation, effortless and without design. There was nothing artificial or theatrical in his manner. He was not being a retired baseball star or general manager of a pennant contender. He was being simply Stan Musial. I couldn't think of anyone else I'd ever met who was so naturally devoid of pretense. I've since discovered that he impresses others in the same way.

We talked for almost two hours. He was attentive during the whole time, yet he never missed a thing that went on in the game. Some action on the field would absorb him momentarily, then he'd return to what he was saying.

From a writer's viewpoint Stan Musial was not a "good interview." Writers like to talk to people who have unusual stories, such as Promuto's; or off-beat personalities, such as Looney's volatile and intense nature; or strong, quotable opinions, like Feller's. Musial gave me none of this. He struck me as an uncomplicated man, without exaggerated moods, with few self-doubts and little tendency to introspection. This makes him sound bland, which he wasn't. He was just a simple, able, genuine and very likable guy. And, as such, a most unusual person. Musial was also a circumspect man. Accustomed to being interviewed, he weighed his words carefully and said exactly what he meant. There was no possibility of trapping him into an unguarded statement. For example, in describing his duties as general manager, he said an important function was to help players with their problems. I asked what type of problems.

He hesitated. "Oh, a player might have a personal problem I can help him with."

What sort of problem?

The words came out of him slowly, each carefully considered. "Oh, he might have some financial difficulties, maybe a housing problem. There might even be some family difficulties."

I asked for a specific example.

He hesitated a long time. Finally, he said, "Gee, I don't see how I can answer that without violating a confidence."

I said I didn't care to know the player's name. I just wanted an example of how a personal problem had been resolved.

After prolonged hesitation, he said, "I d like to answer, but the player would know I was talking about him and it might embarrass him." So Musial did not answer. He wanted to be helpful, he was interested in explaining the role of a general manager. Yet he thought that revealing even a minor confidence would undermine the trust the players had in him and also violate a standard of conduct he had set for himself. A man who behaves this way is often said to have "character."

Musial's uncomplicated nature and his natural cautiousness were repeatedly apparent as he talked about his job as general manager. "I have nothing to do with the on-the-field management of the team," he began, "but in every other respect I run the club and the farm system. I try to run it as loosely as I can. You see, I'm basically a small town boy from Donora, Pennsylvania. And I'm an outdoor guy. I hate being cooped up indoors.

Furthermore, I don't pretend to be any expert in general managing. I learned a certain amount just by watching Bing Devine, who was general manager here during my playing days. When I headed the Physical Fitness Program in Washington, I had some good administrators working for me, and I learned from them. But there is still too much I don't know for me to step in and pretend to run every aspect of this club. We have a good staff. We have people in charge of the farm system, tickets, accounting, public relations, travel arrangements, scouting, groundskeeping, etcetera. I give them a free hand to do their jobs the best they know how. We have meetings so I can keep abreast of what is going on, but I let the staff run it. I know of no other way to do it."

Musial said his particular interest was player personnel—negotiating contracts, solving problems, arranging trades. "I've tried to make our team a happy family. I think the management of this team is closer to the players than on any other club."

If having a happy team was the goal – and becoming World Champions in 1967 surely indicates it was a desirable one – the choice of Musial as general manager was a happy choice. He brought several important qualifications to the job, in addition to his cheerful, confident disposition. He had been a superstar of baseball. He joined the Cardinal organization in 1938, moved up to the parent team at the end of the 1941 season, and played for the next 22 years, except for 1945, when he was in the Army. During those years he set or tied 19 major league records and 29 National League records, including hitting for the most total bases and getting the most extra base hits. Over his career he had 3,630 hits for a .331 lifetime batting average. He batted over .300 for 17 consecutive years. And performance was not Musial's only strong suit. During his years as a player, he was idolized by fans because he was always a gentleman, a sportsman, a credit to the game.

Musial did not say it, indeed he probably could not, but his career as a player had to be an asset to him as general manager. It would be a cocky player, indeed, who would not value the advice of Stan "The Man" Musial.

He certainly commanded the respect of the players, but he did more. "The players understand me and I understand them," he said. "I know how players feel. They want a chance to prove themselves, recognition for their work and money. I understand that and I want to see them get everything that is coming to them. They realized I was on their side and we had no problems."

That is quite a statement. Traditionally the general manager represents the owner, and even the most sports-minded owner wants a good team, large attendance and a profit. The general manager is usually charged with representing the owner's interests, which do not always coincide with the players' desire for a high salary. Musial made it plain he was for the players.

Another thing that aided Musial's efforts to create a happy family was the presence of Red Schoendienst as manager. Schoendienst had been a star second baseman for the Cardinals. His career coincided with Musial's and they had been roommates on the road and close friends.

Now they were running the club together, Schoendienst on the field and Musial in the front office. Every sportswriter has reported that they have worked as a tandem, neither interfering with the other's job, each supporting the other's decisions. When players knew both the manager and general manager were looking out for their interests, happiness just had to result.

One of the happy players on the Cardinals during 1967 was Roger Maris. Much has been written about how Maris hit 61 home runs in 162 games in 1961 to break Babe Ruth's record of 60 home runs in 154 games, then went into a decline with the Yankees. A moody person, he disliked the limelight, became unhappy, succumbed to a succession of injuries and was about to give up baseball when traded to the Cardinals for a little-known third baseman, Charley Smith. With St. Louis, Maris reversed his form to have a good, if not spectacular, year. I asked Musial how he had handled Maris.

"He came in to see me and we talked. I told him we wanted him on the club and that we needed him. We were planning to move Mike Shannon to third base, and we needed Maris badly as a right fielder — and he is an excellent fielder, which many people don't realize. I told him we needed his bat. He was a left-handed hitter, and he would give us the balanced attack that could make us a pennant winner. Finally, I told him that I had come to know St. Louis well and that it was a fine town to play in. I assured him both the fans and the press would be for him — and it has worked out just that way. He's been a real asset." Because he is circumspect, Musial neglected to mention that he offered Maris a contract calling for the same salary he had received in New York, despite his dismal season there in 1966.

Another "difficult" player, Orlando Cepeda, the Cards' star slugger, had been traded to the team by the Giants. Supposedly he was all washed up. I asked Musial about him. "Cepeda is one of the finest hitters in the league and obtaining him made this team. His problem was primarily physical. He didn't feel well and didn't play well. We turned him over to the trainers who worked on him an hour a day. They performed wonders and Cepeda regained his old form. He recognized that he was the team leader and accepted his responsibility. I don't see how he can miss being named the most valuable player."

Musial did a lot more to create the happy pennant winner. "A man plays better when he's happy at home, so I tried to do things for the wives. For example, we offered a babysitting service here at the stadium so the wives could attend more games, and we set up a place for the wives to wait for the players after the game. I think all this helped."

Another important element in the success of the Cardinals, it seemed to me, was Musial's attitude toward baseball. This attitude was revealed when I asked him what had given him the greatest satisfaction in his career. I expected him to mention some of his records or the time he hit four consecutive home runs or the day he had five home runs in a double header. Instead, without hesitation, he said: "Being a big league ballplayer."

I was dissatisfied with the answer. I felt he was being modest and I pressed him.

"Really," he said, "just playing major league ball was my biggest thrill. I'd wanted to be a ballplayer when I was a kid and making it was the biggest thing that ever happened to me."

I could understand his pleasure at making the majors, but after 22 seasons, being a major leaguer must have become "old hat."

"But it didn't. I never spent a boring day on the field. I loved to play. I just couldn't wait to get out on the field. It was a thrill for me every day."

Somehow I couldn't believe him. I said: "Suppose you are 85 years old and your seven-year-old great-grandson, who sees you only as a doddering old man, asks, incredulously, if it was true that you were a major leaguer. What would you tell him?"

Musial smiled broadly at that. The thought of this happening appealed to him. "I'd say that yes, believe it or not, this old wreck played with the St. Louis Cardinals for 22 years."

I asked if he'd tell the boy about his records.

Musial laughed outright at this. "Maybe by that time I would," he said.

I realized that Musial, rather than being modest, was sincere. He had loved to play, every day for 22 years, and he told me that even now he found it difficult to sit in the stands and not play. He compensated in part for this feeling by being a general manager. "I'm still part of the game," he said. I asked if he ever thought of managing. "Never. I don't have the patience. I wouldn't be a good manager."

Musial's attitude toward baseball is contagious. His enthusiasm, his simple joy in the sport undoubtedly had its effect on the team. Like a lot of fans, I'd always thought that many players looked as though they weren't really trying. Perhaps they were, but they didn't look like they were. The Cardinals looked like they were trying, and they looked like they were having fun, too. At least some of the credit had to go to Musial.

About this time Musial said he had to leave. I walked over to another part of the press box to thank Jim Toomey for his help. We talked a bit about some of the things Musial had said. Toomey said, "He does infect people. For example, he never worries as near as I can tell. I remember in the spring we were having a meeting. Some guys were concerned about moving Mike Shannon to third. We all knew he would have to make it there if the team was going to jell. We all worried out loud. Finally Stan was asked his opinion. He said, 'Well, if Shannon doesn't make it at third, we just won't have a third baseman.' This struck everyone as so ludicrous that we all laughed and quit worrying. Shannon has done fine."

There is a word to describe Musial. He has *class*. To me the word encompasses the effortless style with which he does everything, his dignity, the rightness of his actions and demeanor. Other great athletes have had it: Joe Dimaggio, Whitey Ford, Otto Graham, many more.

Musial's class seemed rooted in his simplicity. He loved to play baseball, played it with single-minded devotion and became one of the great players. He could have turned into an egotist, demanding all the privileges of stardom. Yet, he did not. He felt he owed the game a great deal and he wanted to be a credit to it. He played the outfield and first base, according to where he could help the team the most. In his 20th season, after batting under .300 for four years, he launched a conditioning program which brought his average back up to .330 and extended his playing days. As general manager, he was the same "team man," communicating to players the spirit that had made him great.

A popular view of successful men is that they must be great egotists, demanding, self-centered, selfish. There are such men. But there is also Stan Musial, "the man."

DICK WILLIAMS

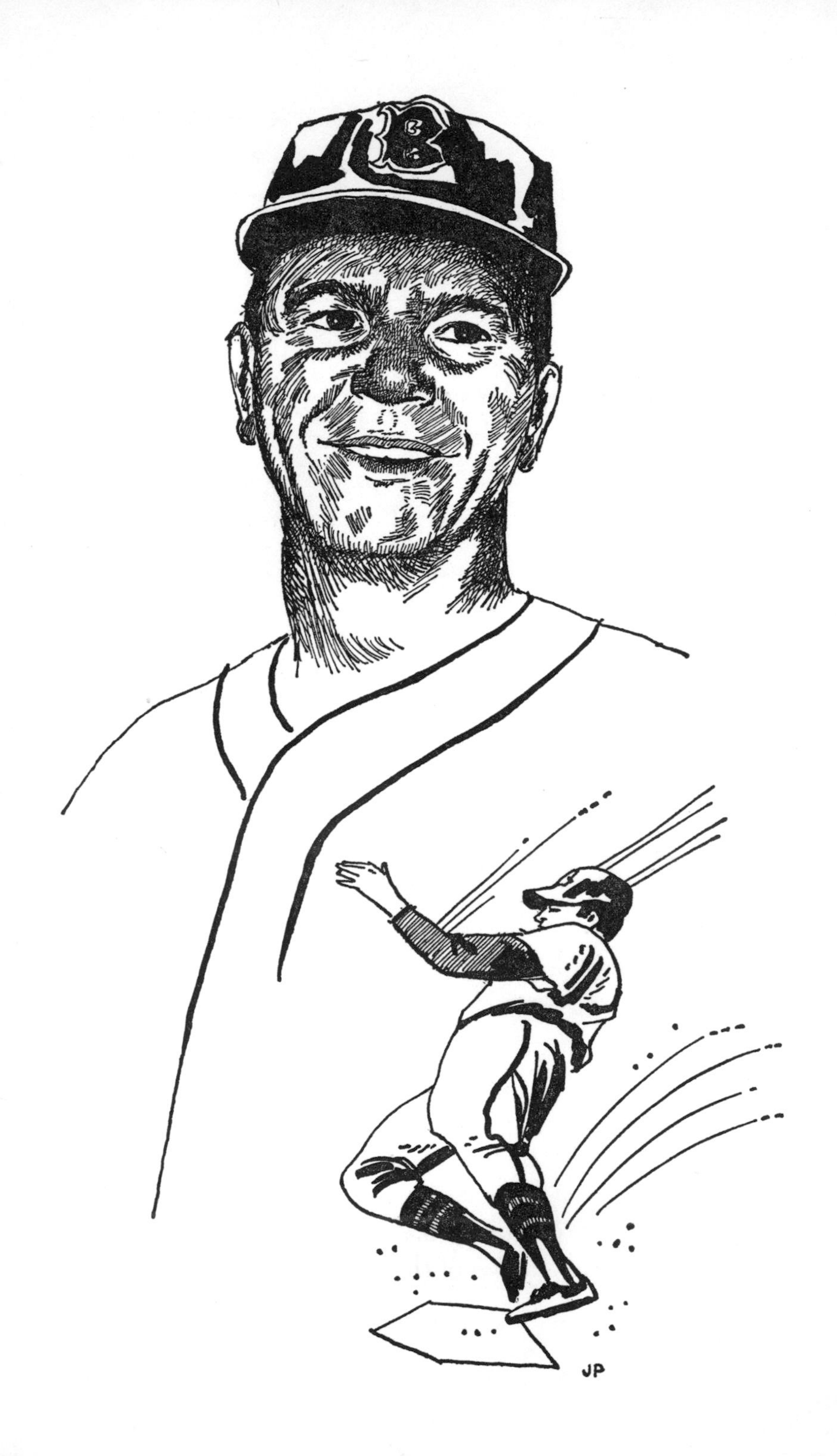
JP

Dick Williams

> *"My job was to make the Red Sox a* team *and to gain the players' respect. If I couldn't do that, I had no right to manage."*

When I decided to talk to Stan Musial, I was quite confident that I had chosen the general manager of the National League's 1967 pennant winners. Picking St. Louis to win in July didn't take too much clairvoyance: the team had a 10-game lead.

The odds were long against my also picking the manager of the winning club in the American League. In July, the American League race was a four-team snarl, and the winner didn't emerge until October 1, the last day of the season. Yet I beat the odds by selecting Dick Williams, manager of the Boston Red Sox.

I wasn't really trying to pick the winners. I just wanted to talk to a field manager in any sport who would be articulate about his job. I decided on a baseball manager, with the advice of the sportswriter who was my consultant. A football coach's job mainly involves plays and strategy. A baseball manager, on the other hand, is more involved with his players' attitudes, more concerned about "handling" them. "A baseball manager will be judged on whether he gets the most out of his players," the sportswriter told me.

My first choice was Bill Rigney of the California Angels. But at that early point in the season, the Angels were stuck in the cellar and sportswriters were predicting Rigney's early dismissal. Rigney seemed to be too big a risk, so I decided not to see him. How wrong could I be? The Angels reversed their form, became contenders for a time and eventually decided the pennant winner by beating Detroit on the last day of the season.

My second choice was Harry Walker of the Pittsburgh Pirates. This team was favored to win the National League pennant. They got off to a slow start, but that appeared to be only a temporary condition. So I tried to arrange the interview. Just as I was getting close, Walker was fired as manager.

I thought of going back to Rigney. Then, on an impulse, I decided that Dick Williams would be good. I'd heard him being interviewed on the radio and was impressed. Besides, the Red Sox were the surprise of baseball. They had finished half a game out of the cellar in 1966. Pre-season forecasts installed them firmly in the cellar in 1967. The odds-makers gave them one chance in a hundred of winning the pennant. Apparently the Red Sox hadn't read the predictions. More than half the season was over and the Sox were holding to first place. Whether or not the team won the pennant, the Sox had shown surprising reversal of form. As the rookie manager, Dick Williams must have had something to do with their success. After all, he had essentially the same team that had done so poorly the year before.

I called Bill Crowley, the Red Sox public relations director. A few days later I received a letter saying Williams would talk to me in his office at Fenway Park prior to the game on August 22.

An accidental piece of good fortune preceded my interview with Williams. Since I was going to Boston, I arranged to have lunch with an old friend, David F. Miller, who is in the insurance business. Dave said he was lunching with someone else, but come along anyhow. The third man turned out to be Buddy LeRoux, trainer for the Red Sox and the Boston Celtics, who was a client of Miller's.

Talking to LeRoux gave me some interesting information. In his career, LeRoux had trained professional baseball, basketball and football players. The basketball player, who runs more than the others, must be in the best condition, LeRoux said. The baseball player has the greatest risk of injury, because he runs and slides and throws and swings in sudden, sharp movements. Football players are usually in excellent condition at the start of a season, right after training camp, but deteriorate as the season progresses. Their injuries are less of a problem for the trainer, despite the roughness of the sport, because they have a whole week to recover before the next game. The baseball player, in contrast, plays the field the next day despite his injury.

Most interesting, considering my coming talk with

Dick Williams, LeRoux said: "Dick Williams is a great believer in conditioning. I think he'll tell you that our conditioning regimen had a great deal to do with the success of the team this year."

LeRoux drove me to Fenway Park after lunch and led the way into the locker room. I was a few minutes early, so he pointed out Williams' office in a corner of the locker room and suggested I wait there.

I had never been in a baseball locker room before. It was a large, sunless room that suggested a basement. Lockers bearing each player's name lined the walls and most were open to reveal neatly pressed uniforms. There was a metal chair before each locker and a small wooden travel chest on top of each. None of the players had arrived yet, so the room was still orderly. Williams' office was perhaps 10 feet square and sparsely furnished. There was a metal desk and chair in the center, a locker with uniforms in the corner and a clothes rack containing more uniforms.

I sat around a few minutes, then a huge man, with a large stomach, came over and asked what I was doing there. I explained and he told me to wait outside. I went over to a chest in the far corner of the locker room and sat down. Some distance to my left Buddy LeRoux had changed into his white trainer's uniform and was donning his socks. This enterprise was interrupted by the appearance of a gray-haired man, sans apparel. This gentleman talked to LeRoux a few minutes, then walked past me into Williams' office. LeRoux came over to explain that was Tom Yawkey, owner of the Red Sox. He had worked out and showered and wanted to dress in the office. He hoped I understood. I did.

The only other interesting inhabitant of the locker room at the time was a boy about 10 years old. He was a handsome, dark-haired lad, very active. He was trying to put on a baseball uniform, a task interrupted frequently by much running about and other shenanigans. For no good reason I guessed this was Williams' son. My guess was confirmed a few moments later when Williams entered and went directly to the boy. He took him aside and appeared to give a father-son lecture. I couldn't hear much of it, but Williams did say, "I want you to apologize and I don't want you to do a thing like that again." Subdued, the boy left the locker room.

Williams looked very natty. He had on a gray checkered jacket, a red handkerchief in the pocket, gray flannel trousers, blue shirt, dark tie and black shoes. He wore his brown hair in a crew cut and kept himself trim. He could have been a player.

He came over, greeted me and, explaining that Yawkey was using his office, sat on the chest beside me. We chatted a few minutes until his office was vacated, then went inside. He closed the door, removed his jacket and shoes and sat behind the desk while I moved up a chair.

Perhaps more than any person I talked to, Dick Williams enjoyed being interviewed. As soon as he discovered I wasn't a sportswriter second guessing his strategy, but someone interested in learning how a baseball manager performs his job, he talked freely. He was excited about managing. It was his first year as a major league manager. He had taken several deliberate steps to renovate the Red Sox, and all of them had worked. He was eager to talk about what had happened. At no time was he boasting about his accomplishments. He was well aware that some kind of miracle was taking place at Fenway Park, and he merely wanted to identify the miracle as no accident.

Williams was a likable, friendly man. Talking about managing, he was like a boy describing a new toy. Yet there was a rough edge to him. He was honest and direct, without any pretense of urbanity or polish. And there was tension in him that fueled the quickness of his mind and his rapid speech. I suspected he had a significant temper, but the temper was obviously well controlled. Hence the tension.

I told him I had selected a baseball manager because strategy seemed such a small part of the job.

"I couldn't agree more. If a manager wins three or four games a year with strategy, he's lucky. I suspect strategy may lose more games than it wins. It's a mistake to overmanage. The game belongs to the players. Only they can win games. It's the manager's job to keep the players in the right frame of mind so they give their best effort over a long season."

How did he accomplish that?

"Each player is an individual. My job is to discover how to handle him. This is a young team. Our average age is only 23. So these fellows take a lot of handling. I had some of them in the minors or my coaches did. Then, I've gotten reports on them from our minor league managers. Still, I've had to learn by a certain amount of trial and error. I've made mistakes, but I think I've discovered what works with each person."

I asked for examples.

"With some, all I have to do is bring them into my office here and have a chat with them. I point out their mistakes and tell them what I expect from them. They shape right up. Another type of fellow has to be benched for a couple of games. That scares him and he goes back ready to give his all. Do that with another guy and he quits on himself. Encourage him and he does his best. Encourage another fellow, he'll get lazy. You have to keep after him every minute. I had to experiment to find out which technique worked with each man. There were some surprises. There was one player I couldn't get next to, no matter how hard I tried. Then one day I called in the reporters and criticized him publicly. That did it. He shaped right up. He's having a great year. You just never know what will work."

Williams listed several specific actions he had taken which transformed the Red Sox from a team "fighting for tenth place" in 1966, as the Boston sportswriters put it, into the 1967 pennant winners.

"I had played with the Red Sox in 1963 and 1964, and I felt I knew a good bit about the team. It was a bad situation, truly deplorable. There was no team spirit. The Red Sox were a group of individual stars looking out for themselves." I asked him to illustrate. "I can think of a typical example. It was the last game of the 1964 season. There was one out and men on second and third as a player came up. He was hit by a pitch. But instead of taking first as he should have, thus loading the bases with one out, he denied he was hit and ended up striking out and ruining the inning. He wasn't thinking of the team and winning. He was thinking only of himself. There was too much of that sort of thing. Everybody called the Red Sox a country club. I think it was.

"When I was named manager at the end of the 1966 season, I decided my job was to make the Red Sox a *team* and to gain the players' respect. If I couldn t do that, I had no right to manage. I decided there weren't going to be any privileged characters on the team. What one did, everyone would do. I didn't care what a guy's batting average was or how many runs he knocked in. All that mattered was how much he contributed to the team.

"My determination to make the Red Sox a team coincided with another observation I'd had as a player. This team was poor in fundamentals. They just weren't making the basic plays of the game. There is a reason for this. Players are maybe four or five years younger today than when I broke in 20 years ago. Many are only 19 and 20 years old and haven't had a long apprenticeship in the minors. They really don't know how to play the game. Today's major league manager has to be a teacher. These are kids. They are still learning.

"So, in spring training everybody went back to school. We spent hours and hours sliding, running the bases, making the throw to the right base, backing up a play, cutting off a throw. I had pitchers practicing covering first base on a hit to the right side of the infield for so long they were ready to drop. We worked on fundamentals until it became automatic to make the right play. Nobody had to think about where to throw the ball. They knew instinctively.

"There were no exceptions to this drill. Everybody did it. Some of the older players thought this was a lot of baloney and balked at being treated like a rookie. They soon found there were no privileged characters on this team. I meant business about this being a *team* that knew its fundamentals. If a man was our biggest star or the rawest rookie, I criticized his mistakes. If he threw to the wrong base, failed to hit the cut off man or missed a sign, he heard about it. If he did it again, he was reprimanded. If he kept repeating the mistake, he was benched. The important thing was that the same rules applied to everyone.

"The training in fundamentals had another advantage. It conditioned the players. When I'd played here, I'd felt too many men weren't in top physical shape. This contributed to injuries and marred performances. One of my first acts upon being named manager was to talk to Buddy LeRoux, who I think is the best trainer in the business. We went over the whole roster and decided the best playing weight for each man. When we sent out the contracts, we specified how much each player should weigh when he reported for spring training. We laid down the rule that a man would be fined $50 a day for each pound he was overweight. If a man was 10 pounds overweight, he was given a certain period in which to lose it. If he didn't, it cost him $500 a day. The Red Sox showed up at spring training in the best shape they have ever been in. Take George Scott. He likes to eat and he puts on weight which slows him down. He was overweight, but he discovered I meant business. I benched him until he took off the weight, and it cost him money. But he is having his best year.

"When spring training started, we had players with their weight under control. Those who had injuries were asked to perform special exercises over the winter. Then all the training in fundamentals worked wonders. The running, sliding and throwing got the Red Sox into top physical shape."

All the sports pundits had relegated the Red Sox to the cellar because their pitching was supposed to be weak. What had he done about that?

"At the start of spring training, I announced that no sore-armed pitchers were going north with the team. I knew we didn't have great pitching, so what we lacked in quality, we had to make up in quantity. There just wasn't any room on the roster for a pitcher who couldn't contribute to the team. And, we didn't have a single sore arm when we reached Boston."

Did he mean the arms were still sore, only the pitchers didn't complain?

"No, there weren't any sore arms. Oh, a couple of fellows went to the minors to work out some soreness. The rest had sound arms."

I didn't understand. If a pitcher had a sore arm, what could a manager do about it?

"I don't pretend to be an expert on pitching, but I believe, and Buddy LeRoux does, too, that if a pitcher's legs and body are in condition, his arm will be also. Suppose a pitcher has a sore leg. He can't make his normal motion and puts an extra strain on his arm. Next thing you know he has a bad arm. Or, maybe he is overweight. Compensating for the poundage, he strains his arm. We set out to relieve sore arms by strengthening legs. We ran the pitchers to death. We set up special drills. They spent hours covering first base and backing up throws to the plate or third. We had them shagging flies. We ran them and ran them. Their tongues were hanging out, but it worked. Legs were in shape and arms became healthy.

"Sal Maglie, our pitching coach, had all the pitchers break in gradually. No hard throwing. Just toss the ball lightly for five minutes the first day. This was increased gradually so as not to strain the arm. Pretty soon everybody was throwing hard. I'll tell you, we may not have the best pitching, but we have healthy pitchers."

Williams started to change into his uniform.

"All of this conditioning and stress on fundamentals contributed to teamwork. Everyone was healthy and everyone contributed to the team and its success. The Red Sox became one for all and all for one."

It seemed to me that more must be needed to make a winning club. I'd always thought mental attitude vital to baseball. A baseball player is a huge success if he fails seven out of 10 times at the plate. That makes him a .300 hitter. No other sport, perhaps no other endeavor, asks the performer to endure such a high failure rate. I mentioned this and asked how a player keeps from getting down on himself?

"Look, a man can go 0 for 4 and make such a big

contribution to the team that he thinks he went 3 for 4. So he didn't get a hit, but maybe he saved a run with his glove. Or, maybe he hit to the right side of the infield so as to advance a runner. Sure, the batter was out. The box score will never reflect his contribution, but he helped the team win. He knows it and I know it. Maybe he hustled down to first to prevent a double play. There are many ways a good team man can beat the other guy. My job is to let him know I appreciate his effort, even though he went hitless.

"The goal is to have every person putting out 115 per cent, not 110 per cent. When you have enthusiastic fans as we do in Boston, that helps players put out that extra effort. But it's my job, too, to do whatever is necessary to keep players putting out all the time. For example, every team has trouble winning in Los Angeles. We played there early in the season, won the first game, then dropped the next two. The trouble is that there is too much diversion in Los Angeles. There is a lot of nightlife, things to do and places to go. I figured that was the trouble. So, the next time we played in Los Angeles, I instituted a bed check. Anyone not in bed at a specified hour was fined. So what happened? We lost the first two games anyhow. We were having a bad road trip, and we were discouraged. After the second loss, I said, 'Let's go out on the town and have some fun.' We did — and you know what happened? We lost the third straight the next day for a 2–7 road trip. But we came home loose as a goose. We got hot and we have stayed hot. Sometimes you never know what will work."

The miracle Williams wrought in Boston was no accident. He set out, quite deliberately, to create a *team* that was in top physical condition, well grounded in fundamentals, and which valued winning above any individual performance. But if he had explained how the miracle happened, I still had little insight into Williams, the miracle worker. He struck me as a nice guy. Like Musial, he seemed to be without egotism. If pride goes before a fall, Dick Williams would remain upright.

I asked him to tell me about his baseball career.

"I came up through the Dodger organization. I learned all my baseball there, and I'm still using Dodger methods. I signed with the Dodgers out of high school in 1947. The next year I was at Santa Barbara, California, and in 1949 and 1950 I was with Fort Worth and Dallas in the American Association. In 1951, I came up to the Dodgers as an outfielder. I was doing very well, and in 1952 I was to be the regular left fielder. Then I separated my shoulder and that finished me as an outfielder. I couldn't throw the ball across the locker room.

"I should have quit, I suppose, but baseball was all I knew how to do and all I wanted to do. I went back to the minors and learned to play the infield where I wouldn't have to make the long throw. I spent the next year, that would be 1953, in Montreal. I spent part of the next year with the Dodgers, then went down to St. Paul. In '55 I was in Fort Worth and had a pretty good year. Since the Dodgers had no room for me on the team, I asked to be traded.

"I was sold to Baltimore in 1956. I was with Cleveland in 1957, then back in Baltimore in '58. The next two years I was in Kansas City, where I had my best year, batting .288 with 16 homers and 75 RBIs. In '61 and '62 I was back in Baltimore. In '63 I was traded to Houston on paper, then sent to Boston where I played two years and retired at the end of the 1964 season.

"I wasn't a great player. I was a utility man, playing every position except pitcher and catcher. I sort of hung on by my grubby fingertips, helping a young club that was rebuilding. As soon as a better player came along, I moved on. After the '64 season, the Red Sox asked me if I'd go to Seattle as a player-coach. It kept me in baseball, so I did. In 1965 I got lucky and was named manager. It was a good team with a lot of these same players on it, and in 1966 we won the Governor's Cup by winning the International League playoff.

"I was fortunate to play under some excellent managers, particularly Paul Richards, Charley Dressen and Bobby Bragan. They are three different types of managers. If you put them in the same room, they'd disagree on most everything. But I learned something from each. I can't separate what I learned from whom, but I know all three influenced me. As a player I'd ask questions, not as criticism, but seeking information. Why did they make a particular move? How did they know when to lift the pitcher? There were many questions. I listened and I learned. When I became a manager I made use of it."

Williams played with the Baltimore Orioles on three separate occasions while Paul Richards was manager. I remembered from living in Baltimore that Williams had been a popular player and that Richards favored him because he was a hustler, a team man, an example and a steadying influence on a young team. Williams apparently had the same effect on the young Red Sox club. And since he had played 13 seasons in the majors by being a team man, it was only natural for him to insist that the Red Sox could succeed only if they played as a team.

As Williams and I talked, we were frequently interrupted by his son, who came in and out of the office. He couldn't find his socks. He wanted a soda and brought his father one and served me. Williams was distracted by his son yet patient with him. I remarked that the boy seemed just like my 10-year-old son and that it must be a big thrill for him to suit up and be around a big league team. "Yes," Williams said, "he likes it and I'm glad to have him do it. But he gets a little cocky once in awhile."

The boy left the room and we resumed talking. I asked what was the hardest part of managing.

"Knowing when to take out the pitcher. I don't profess to know anything about pitching. I can't tell anyone how to throw a slider or curve. I leave all that to Sal Maglie. All I can tell a pitcher is to throw hard and keep the ball low. Early Wynn was the only successful high ball pitcher I ever knew. I check with the catcher every inning to see if the pitcher has his stuff. Then, if he gets in a jam, I try to go with the percentages. No pitcher likes to be taken out, but I tell them to throw as hard as they can for as long as they can, then I'll bring in somebody else. The day of the nine-inning pitcher is gone."

At this point we both heard the sounds of a ruckus outside the office. There were some shouts and a large bang. I didn't think much about it, but Williams was concerned. A moment later, the door opened and in bolted his son in such a rage he could only cry in frustration. Williams looked at him, obviously thinking what to do. He turned to me as if to say something, then looked back at his son.

Very quietly he said, "Go take a shower."

"But I had a shower," the boy protested.

"Take another one. Change into your street clothes and sit in the stands. You may be sitting there permanently from now on."

Crushed, the lad picked up his clothes and fled the room crying.

Like most fathers, Williams was upset over having to discipline his son. "I've got to teach him that if he is going to kid around out there, he has got to take it as well as dish it out."

We talked a little more after that, while Williams prepared his lineups for the day's twi-night doubleheader with Washington. (Boston won both.) Soon it was time for him to go out on the field, and he excused himself. I left his office. After going over to thank Buddy LeRoux for his assistance, I walked out of the locker room. In my last glimpse of Williams, I saw him bending over to talk quietly to his son.

I admired the way Williams had handled his son. If the situation had been reversed and I was being interviewed while my son was cutting up, I probably would have blown up in anger. Williams was annoyed, but he kept his temper and used the situation to teach his son a lesson. That, I thought, could be a large clue to his success as a manager.

BILLY CASPER

JP

Billy Casper

*"I never think about money.
I think about winning.
Winning is everything."*

THE HIGHEST PAID athletes in the world are American professional golfers. Arnold Palmer and Jack Nicklaus earn around one million dollars a year from prize money, endorsements and business activities, some, but not all, related to golf. Probably no other golfers are in the million-a-year class, but a significant number earn a great deal of money. By mid-September, 1967 seven golfers had earned more than $100,000 in prize money, and the tournament schedule was far from complete. All of the top ten money winners, and other golfers as well, supplement their tournament winnings with income from endorsements, lessons and public appearances.

Golf is big business. Major cities hold one or more golf tourneys offering first prizes of $20,000 to $50,000. Television carries two to four hours of golf every week.

Millions play golf, either in private clubs, or on public links or driving ranges. The popularity of golf as a sport is somewhat surprising. The game demands a lot from the players. Before ever going out on the course, a golfer must make a sizeable investment in clubs, balls, bag, shoes and other paraphernalia. Membership in a club can cost thousands of dollars. (Golf has, indeed, always been associated with affluence – and perhaps that has something to do with its popularity.) Playing golf requires a large block of time, which should lessen its appeal – but doesn't. Finally, golf is a difficult game, requiring precise form and enormous concentration and mental discipline. All of these may be obstacles, but there are millions of men and women determined to surmount them.

The popularity of professional golf and the fame and fortune professional golfers have won made it a logical choice for this book. But there was another reason why I wanted to interview a golfer. Golf is the only major sport in which a man plays against himself. The professional golfer may be beaten by a competitor who turns in a better score. But that competitor will have done nothing directly to damage the other man's performance. In baseball, a batter is beaten by a good pitcher. In football, basketball, hockey, tennis, nearly every other sport, the outcome is determined in a direct, personal clash between the participants. Not so in golf. If Arnold Palmer is playing Jack Nicklaus and misses a six-foot putt, Palmer has only himself to blame. Nicklaus did nothing overt to help or to hinder him. Golf is a solo performance. I wanted to talk to a pro, to find out if playing this solo game made him a different kind of man than the professional baseball, football and basketball player.

I tried to arrange an interview with Arnold Palmer, but his public relations representative said Palmer was doing his own books and couldn't be in this one. Nicklaus and Gary Player, the other two members of the "Big Three" of golfdom, are represented by the same public relations firm and are also authors, so there seemed little chance of interviewing them.

Badly in need of advice, I called Dick Aultman, editor of *Golf Digest*. I explained that I wanted to interview a golfer who was well known, one who would be articulate about himself and his sport. Aultman suggested, as his first choice, Billy Casper.

I'd heard of Casper, of course, but since I don't play golf and don't follow it as closely as some other sports, I was surprised to learn from Aultman that Casper was the second leading money winner of all time. Only Palmer ranked ahead of him. Without doubt, Casper qualified as a leading player.

With help from Aultman, I arranged the interview, talking to Gary Warren, who is Casper's assistant and travels with him. As a final check, I had to call Casper's public relations counsel in San Francisco for approval. It turned out that Casper was planning books, too, but if I mentioned that in this book, it would be okay for Casper to see me. The meeting was to take place in Upper Montclair, New Jersey, where Casper was competing in the Thunderbird Golf Classic.

I was to arrive at one o'clock on Friday, after Casper

had completed the second round. About midmorning I left my home in Connecticut and crossed the Tappan Zee Bridge over the Hudson River into New Jersey. After many miles on the Garden State Parkway, I asked the attendant at a toll booth which exit I should use.

The attendant was a friendly, paunchy fellow. "It's Exit 153," he said. "I hope you can park. I hear it's pretty crowded."

I said I hoped so, too, because I had to interview one of the golfers.

"Why don't you interview me?" he said. "I'm a golfer."

I asked how his game was.

"Oh, great. I almost break a hundred."

Casper had finished the second round early and had left the club by the time I got there. I made several frantic phone calls, in a state of frustration and agitation, my conversation with the toll booth man beginning to seem prophetic. Finally, I talked to Gary Warren and discovered that Casper was in Elizabeth, New Jersey, where he was staying at a friend's house.

Billy Casper is five-feet-ten inches tall, weighs 175 pounds, has brown wavy hair, strong, even teeth, a ruddy complexion and soft blue eyes. He looks like your next-door neighbor, a friendly, easygoing chap, ready to lend you a screwdriver any time you need it and never ask for its return. The impression is total, from his shy smile and soft voice to his casual clothes – when I saw him he was wearing a yellow sweater, khaki pants, blue socks and no shoes. There is nothing aggressive about him, and he seems in fact to be so much the nice guy who wants to please that I wondered how he could be so successful in an intensely competitive sport like professional golf. But I soon realized that his placid disposition reflects a strong self-discipline. He is "cool," unruffled by questions, extremely self-contained, because he is an introspective man. He has thought a lot about himself and about golf and his role in it.

In 1967, Billy Casper had been a pro for 12 years, and in that time, he had won $705,371.21 in prize money. This ranked second to Palmer's $906,844.11 and ahead of Nicklaus' $684,112.83. Casper had twice won the United States Open, probably the world's premier tourney, along with 34 other tournaments, a winning total exceeded only by Palmer. In 1966, he had been golf's leading money winner and been named Golfer of the Year. In 1967, he already had won $110,000 in prize money, but that was the least of his income. He represented a major sporting goods company, two clothing manufacturers and a brand of golf shoes. He didn't tell me, but his earnings undoubtedly amounted to several hundred thousand dollars a year, which enabled him to employ a staff consisting of Gary Warren, a business manager, an attorney, a tax attorney, a secretarial service, a bookkeeper and a caddy.

Why wasn't he more well-known, since he was the second best money winner in the game? The *New York Times,* in its thorough coverage of the Thunderbird Classic, had run large photographs of Palmer, Nicklaus and Player in action, but Casper had received only the barest mention, even though he was just two strokes off the lead.

There was no hint of envy in his answer. "I think television has had a lot to do with the popularity of Palmer, Nicklaus and Player. Their shows, *Big Three Golf* and *Palmer & Player Challenge,* have run for a number of years. This is bound to make them better known to the public. And they've won a number of major tournaments. Palmer has won the Masters four times, the U.S. Open once and the British Open twice. These are the major championships and sportswriters make a point of writing about them and the people who win them. I always felt that after I won my second U.S. Open in 1966 I would receive more publicity, but it didn't work out that way, although some sportswriters have listed Palmer, Nicklaus and Casper as the so-called 'Big Three.' After all, Player hasn't won a tourney since 1965. Finally, I'd say their press agent has a lot to do with their popularity. He's earned his money."

I asked if being "colorful" led to popularity

"I don't think so. I don't have any gimmicks to win the crowds over to me. I try to let my golf speak for me. That's what Ben Hogan did and he was extremely popular. Jack Nicklaus doesn't use gimmicks. His golf game does all the talking. Now Palmer is different. He plays excellent golf, of course, but he also plays to the crowds and they appreciate that. Some other members of the tour play the crowds. Doug Sanders does it with his attire and Chi Chi Rodrigues with the different things he does. But a fellow like Julius Boros just plays golf. There's room for both types of players. Personally, I've patterned myself after Hogan more than anyone."

Would he like to be more popular?

"Oh, yes, I don't think there is any doubt that popularity is valuable. A popular, well-known player is asked to endorse more products. He commands larger fees for exhibitions and appearances. But there is a disadvantage to popularity. Nicklaus and Palmer follow a very strenuous schedule and I wouldn't want that. I couldn't do justice to my family, my game and the people I represent. I have a wife, daughter and two sons, and I want to spend time with them. I went to Vietnam last year to visit the troops. I visit the wounded in hospitals when I can. I make talks to church groups and I try to work with young golfers. All of this is important to me, and I want time to do it."

Why did he need Gary Warren to travel with him?

"Many things come up when you get to a tourney. There are your travel arrangements, accommodations, interviews such as this one. I can't think about these things and do justice to my game. I need someone to relieve me of all these details. My wife used to travel with me and take care of all this. But about a year ago, she decided she needed to stay home with the children, so I hired Gary. A step like this is a reflection of the growth of professional golf. When I started on the tour 12 years ago, the prize money for the whole tour totaled $750,000. This year it is $4.5 million. Next year it will be $5.2 million. Last year three players won $100,000 or over. This year seven have already. Next year there will be more. I don't think anyone ever expected golf to grow so big. The outstanding players, and by that I mean the top ten money winners, are doing extraordinarily well financially, but they aren't the only ones. Last week I came in third in Philadelphia and picked up a check for $6,100. That's a lot of money. Dan Sykes came in second at Westchester (New York) and won $30,000. Even if a player doesn't win, he can still do very well by just placing in the money."

Golf has always been a source of income to Casper, and the need for money has shaped his career. "I was born in San Diego. My parents were poor. Both my mother and father have always worked. When I was young, we lived in Mexico for several years on a ranch owned by my grandfather. He and my father scratched out a three-hole golf course in the cow pasture and I started playing when I was four-and-a-half years old. We moved back to California when I was six, but I kept on playing golf. I just grew up with the game.

"I played other sports. Baseball was my first love. I really wanted to be a professional baseball player. But I couldn't make any money at baseball, while I could pick up a few dollars caddying at the golf course. I needed the money for clothes, dates and other things, so I gravitated to golf more and more.

"I liked golf and I was just naturally good at it. In high school in Chula Vista (south of San Diego) I shot in the low seventies and high sixties."

I expressed surprise that he had been so good so young. Had he had good instruction?

"No. I've had only six lessons in my life, all in high school. It was then that I switched from the full-finger grip to the Vardon or overlapping grip. I don't know why golf was so easy for me, but I can tell you what I believe.

Everyone who lives on earth has a particular skill or talent that he is blessed with. Unfortunately, most people never discover their talent and work to perfect it."

Casper went on with his story.

"When I was 16 or 17, I decided to be a golf pro. I didn't know how or when, but I knew this was what I'd be. The summer before I graduated from high school, in 1950, I had caddied for a fellow who had been captain of the Notre Dame golf team. He wanted me to go to Notre Dame and arranged for me to be accepted. I spent the next winter in South Bend, Indiana, but I just didn't like the snow and cold weather and went back to San Diego. I thought I'd get my game in shape and maybe turn pro.

"The Korean War had started. I joined the Navy for three years. I was most fortunate. I was assigned to operate and build golf driving ranges for the Navy in the San Diego area, which hardly qualifies me as a war hero.

"I turned pro while in the Navy. Again it was need for money that forced the decision. I'd married and my wife was expecting our first child. My seaman's wages were hardly enough to live on. Besides, the golf courses in the area had started to charge green fees. By turning pro, I avoided paying the green fees and I made a few dollars. I played in a lot of local tournaments with $50 and $100 purses. Fortunately, my officers approved of my playing and gave me time off.

"The Navy also led to my joining the tour. One of my close friends in the Navy was a Chief Petty Officer. He was a pretty good golfer himself, and he wanted me to join the tour. Since he knew I couldn't afford to, he talked a couple of businessmen into financing me. The deal was that these men would pay my expenses on the tour for three years. I agreed to pay back all the money they advanced and 30 per cent of my winnings over that period. They outfitted me with a car and trailer and in June, 1955, accompanied by my wife and baby daughter, I joined the PGA tour. I won $33.33 in my first tourney, the Western Open. It was quite remarkable to place in the money in your first tournament.

"The rest of that year I won about $4,000, but my expenses were about $12,000. The next year, which was a full year on the tour, I won $18,733, which made me the twelfth money winner. In 1957, I won $20,807 and in 1958, I earned $41,323. So those fellows who backed me got 30 per cent of my winnings, plus their money back. They made a pretty good investment. I never objected to sharing with them. I was grateful for their backing. I could never have gone on tour without them. I was just glad I made money. I don't know how I would ever have paid them back."

Casper's brief account made his career as a pro golfer sound easy. It wasn't.

"In my first tourney, I found out that I had as good shots as some of the best names, men like Cary Middlecoff, Mike Souchak and Ted Kroll. But they knew something I didn't. They knew how to *score* the ball. You see, there is more to golf than just hitting the ball. A lot of preparation has to go into every shot. You have to plan where to hit the ball, particularly when you get around the greens. It took a lot of practice and just plain experience for me to learn to score the ball so that even if I wasn't playing well, I could still score well."

I didn't understand what he meant by "scoring the ball."

"It's a lot of things. It means being able to read the greens so you know where to place the ball for the easiest putt. Scoring the ball means being able to get out of trouble. It means knowing your own capabilities, your limits and capacities. I learned never to try a shot I couldn't make. Let me give you an example. The twenty-second hole on the Upper Montclair course here is a par 5, 530 yarder to an elevated green surrounded by a lake. My tee shot went to a point which gave me a chance to make the green in two. It was a temptation to go for it, and maybe some of the time I would. But I just felt today that I couldn't make it, and I knew that if I didn't, I'd be in the water for a bogey or worse. So, I played short of the lake, reached the green in three and putted for a birdie.

"Not everyone has this philosophy. Some go full-bore all the time. They'd charge across the lake and win or lose. Arnold Palmer is this way. He is full-bore all the time. He doesn't know any other way to play, and you can't quarrel with his success. But I'm not that way. Sometimes I'd chance that second shot and sometimes I wouldn't. It depends on how I feel. But I've been one of the consistent players through the years, and I think my attitude accounts for it. I have a sound knowledge of my own golf game."

Casper spoke of the same faculty for "scoring the ball"

in different terms when I asked him what made some golfers more successful than others.

"The same 10 golfers win most of the tournaments year after year, despite the improved caliber of play. These days only seven or eight strokes separate first from last. Years ago the separation was twice that. We have more ties today and play offs. Everybody is a good golfer. Every person on the tour has good shots or he wouldn't be there. The difference between the 10 men who win most of the money and the rest is *course management,* the ability to think yourself around the course.

"Let me give you an example. There's a hole on this course which is about 370 yards, par 4. There are trees on the left and the fairway slopes sharply downward to the right. Today the wind was blowing from right to left. Now it is a temptation to stand at the tee and bang away for distance. But I didn't believe this was smart. Just before the slope there is a flat mound. It seemed to me wiser to play a short tee shot to the mound. I'd have a level lie and be able to get off a second shot that played the wind properly and had the right spin to stop dead on the green. That's the way I played it and got a birdie. You see, if I had taken a long tee shot, I'd have had a downhill lie which would make the approach shot difficult. Course management means knowledge of the course and your own capability. It means keeping the ball in play so you are always in a position to try for a birdie. Lots of players have fantastic games, but they can't think a lick. Course management will mean three or four shots in a tourney, and three or four shots is the difference between first and tenth money."

I asked who he considered to be the great thinkers of golf.

"Ben Hogan was probably the greatest. Nicklaus is very good. Del Finsterwald never won too many tournaments, but he was a great course manager. And I think myself. It has been said by many players that I am the best of those currently on the tour."

I asked about Palmer as a course manager.

"Palmer is sheer guts and brute force. He goes full bore all the time, for he is blessed with the talent to do the things he thinks he can. He has tremendous desire. In other words, he has all the ingredients, plus boldness. Walter Hagen was probably the only other in history who played golf the way Palmer does. He's a wonder."

Casper's words reflected his respect for Palmer, but at the same time he feels strong competition with Palmer. He, too, has great desire.

"I set goals for myself. As soon as I reach one goal, I set a new one. I'm not going to tell you my current goals, but I'll tell you some I've reached. I wanted to be an outstanding golfer, and I wanted to win a championship, which I did after 13 months on the tour. Winning the U.S. Open was a goal. I reached that in 1959. Then I wanted to win another U. S. Open. I did that in 1966. I wanted to be the leading money winner, and I did that in 1966. And I wanted to win the San Diego Open in my home town, which I did last year."

I asked if being the leading all-time money winner was a goal.

"I don't think that's possible. Arnold is well ahead of me, and he and I will be playing for at least another 10 years. But Jack Nicklaus is a lot younger than either of us. He'll play longer and pass us both, I think."

Casper's desire showed in other ways. "When I joined the tour, I had faults. I was a chronic hooker. I had to work hard to correct it. I didn't read the greens well, and I didn't score well. I had to work on that. For a long time I was known for my short game and putting, but I was weak on the tees. But you can't be a consistent winner unless you have a solid, well-rounded game. So, I practiced an awful lot, at least eight hours a day. If a shot went bad, I tried to figure why, then worked to correct it. I did it all myself. I never asked anyone for help. I'm self-taught.

"A couple of years ago, I realized that one trouble with my game was my weight. I weighed 220 pounds — too much. So I forced myself on a diet and got down to 175 pounds. After that my earnings really went up."

They did, indeed. Casper won $61,842 in 1962. The next year he was out several weeks with an injured hand and won only $32,726. In 1964, after losing 45 pounds, his earnings jumped to $90,653, then to $99,931 and to $121,944 in 1966, highest on the tour. In 1967, he had already won $111,000. Casper's diet won him a good bit of notoriety, for he was addicted to strange foods such as buffalo meat, which he believed controlled his weight yet kept his strength up.

Casper feels that golf is a unique game. "It is the only sport where you rely solely upon yourself for what you do, and it is the only sport in which spectators are permitted to mingle with the participants. As a result, golf requires tremendous concentration and self-discipline.

Your last shot can't be changed. You must forget it and concentrate on the next one. Younger players tend to fret about their bad shots, and their whole game is affected. You can't do this. You have to control your mind. Of course, you have to care about that bad shot. I'm basically a perfectionist. I want to do anything as well as I can. If I make a bad shot, I try to discover why and learn from the mistake, but I don't want to get down on myself because of the error. When you are playing a round, you have enough to think about without worrying about the last shot."

I suggested that concentration must really be difficult. Golf is a slow game. A player shoots from the tee, then walks for several minutes to the fairway before resuming the game. His mind must wander during that time.

"While walking to the next shot, I usually chat with the other players or my caddy. The conversation is usually quite light, so it can be dropped at any time. I get into no esoteric discussions, that's for sure. Actually, I never forget the game. I put it into the back of my mind for a moment or two. Then, before I get to the ball, I think about all the factors involved in the next shot – my lie, the distance to the green, location of the pin, the wind, the type of green. There are many factors that go into the next shot. I'm concentrating solely upon it.

"If something happens to disturb my concentration, it can be very upsetting. For example, I was in the final round of the Carling Open at the Board of Trade Country Club in Toronto. I was leading and first prize was $35,000. On one of the holes, I'd made a bad tee shot and was faced with a difficult shot to the green. At that moment, one of the spectators grabbed me and said, 'Remember two years ago?' That shattered my concentration. It gave me something entirely extraneous to think about. I was very sharp with the fellow. I said, 'Buddy, I can't remember two years ago. I'm in this golf tourney trying to win $35,000.' The incident took maybe 10 or 15 seconds, but I was upset, mostly because I'd been so sharp with the fellow who, after all, hadn't meant any harm. Largely because of the incident, I bogied the hole. But I went on to win the tourney and everything worked out okay."

I said there must be a lot of pressure involved in $35,000 stakes.

"Pressure is everything in golf. If it wasn't for pressure, I couldn't play. It's that way with all the top players. Pressure brings out the best in them. If I'm just playing a round for fun, I don't play well. I need a challenge. I need something to strive for, whether it is 25 cents or $25,000.

"Yet I never think about money. I think about winning. Winning is everything. If I can't win, I try to be second. If not second, third and so on. A lot of golfers, if they see they can't win, they give up. Not me. If I feel myself coasting, I get right on myself. You never know what will happen in this game. Last year in the Open, Palmer was leading by seven strokes with nine holes to go, and he's famous for his great clutch finishes. So, trailing by so much, I merely tried for second. I made up a stroke or two, but when I got to the fifteenth, he was still leading by five strokes with four holes to play. Well, I birdied the fifteenth and sixteenth, and he bogied both.

That was four shots made up right there. He bogied the seventeenth and I parred it. We both parred the eighteenth for a tie. I had shot a 32 on the back nine, just trying for second money. In the playoff the next day, he took an early two stroke lead, but I overcame it and won by two strokes. You just never can tell what will happen in this game."

I said I'd observed that players seem to go in streaks. They'll win two or three tourneys, then fade for a while. What caused that?

"I wish I knew. It is true that everyone's game runs in streaks. I guess there are times when you are better in tune with what you are trying to accomplish. I think rest has a lot to do with it. If I play too much, I get tired of playing and lose the power to concentrate. I realize I need a rest. I take off for a couple of weeks and go fishing, or I do some church work. I don't even touch a club. When I return, I'm refreshed and my game improves."

Casper's reference to church work indicates his strong religious feelings. He is a Mormon, a convert in 1966, and a devout one. "I feel I'm a missionary of the Gospel of Jesus Christ of the Latter Day Saints," he said. "As I travel, people see the life I lead, the way I conduct myself and the examples I set. I try to live so as not to be all wrapped up in material things. I try not to forget what I'm here for, and that is to put my perfected talent in the service of my fellow man. I use all my free time to talk to church groups and young people. Golf is a wonderful vehicle to spread goodwill around the world."

Casper's hostess was putting dinner (elk meat for

Casper) on the table, so it was time for me to leave. He accompanied me to my car, and then turned the tables on me by saying: "I enjoyed being interviewed. You strike me as an honest writer."

Surprised, I reacted cynically, saying I might be further ahead if I weren't.

"Don't believe it," he said. "Be honest and it will pay off in the long run."

Talking to Casper, I'd wanted to find out if golf, as an individual sport, required different attitudes than team sports. Casper made me believe it does not. He spoke of desire, practice, concentration and ability to play well under pressure. These were the same ingredients for success most of the athletes who play team sports had mentioned. And Casper seemed the same likable, well-integrated person as the team players I'd met.

Before I left, I asked Casper how he thought he'd do in the Thunderbird.

"I feel I can win. I'm playing well. If I can stay within a couple of shots, I think I'll win. Two or three shots is nothing in 72 holes."

As it turned out, Casper was tied with six others at the end of 36 holes. He was a stroke off the lead at the end of the third round. As late as the eleventh hole in the final round, he was leading. Then, he "blew," took a 40 on the final nine and came in third. The winner came on with a hard charge. His name was Arnold Palmer.

I was concerned about Casper's bad final round, because immediately after leaving him I'd become ill. I spent three days in bed feeling as if trucks were running over me. I wondered if I had infected Casper and ruined his game, so I called his public relations man in San Francisco.

"No," he said, "Billy didn't become ill and he didn't play badly, but the most incredible things happened to his shots. One hit a tree, another went into the crowd. It seemed everything that could go wrong with a golf shot did."

Casper's next tourney was the Arcan Open in Scotland. First money was $55,000, the richest in golf. Casper tied Gay Brewer for the lead at the end of regulation play, but lost the playoff by four strokes. A tough break, I thought. But it was difficult to generate too much sympathy for a nice guy who had just won $15,000 as a second prize.

CAZZIE RUSSELL

Cazzie Russell

"This year I've got more confidence. I know what I can do, and I'm going to relax and do it."

The Old Madison Square Garden, perhaps the most famous arena in the world, was a huge rectangular cavern, with hundreds of rows of seats in a series of tiers. Shorn of spectators, the Garden seemed even more cavernous. A dozen Knicks were shooting baskets and knots of photographers and reporters were talking, but no activity, no voice seemed capable of filling the arena. Emptiness dominated everything and reduced all talk to hushed tones.

The Knicks' publicity man, Jim Wergeles, called to Cazzie Russell out on the floor and asked him to come over to the side to meet me. Russell wore a ragbag gray sweatsuit that had been stretched out of shape. Underneath he had on still another sweatshirt, and perspiration ran in rivulets off his face. Wergeles introduced us and

Russell told me to stick around until after the practice. His manner was brusque, even surly – but, I realized later, he was simply intent on the practice.

Cazzie Russell had been the top collegiate player of the 1965–1966 season at the University of Michigan. He was the first player selected in the National Basketball Association draft early in 1966, and the Knicks signed him to a handsome contract with a bonus of $200,000. Russell was immediately touted as a candidate for instant stardom. But he sat on the bench the first half of the season, even though the Knicks were a young team in the process of rebuilding, and in his statements to reporters, he made it quite plain that he was unhappy not to be playing.

I thought it would be revealing to talk to a college star who had completed his rookie year in the NBA, and Russell seemed a perfect choice. His unhappy first-year experience would, I felt, have sharpened his feelings about what it's like to be a rookie. I also wanted to talk to a college star who was just turning pro. As it happened, the Knicks had again signed a top college star in 1967, a player almost as highly regarded as Russell. This was Walt Frazier, who had led Southern Illinois University to victory in the 1967 National Invitation Tournament. Southern Illinois was a large school, but because of its schedule, it was considered a "small college" in basketball rankings. Yet during the season Southern Illinois defeated such powers as Louisville, Wichita, St. Louis and Southern Methodist, and then confounded everyone by winning the NIT tourney. Frazier, the team's playmaking guard, was named the most valuable player in the tournament. He had a year of college eligibility left but was drafted by the Knicks and signed to a bonus reported to be $90,000. Talking to a first and second year man who were on the same team, would, I thought, heighten the comparison between them.

The interviews were easy to arrange. The Knicks were holding a press day for sportswriters and photographers at Madison Square Garden, the day before the first regular season game, and I was invited to it. Frazier had hurt his ankle in an exhibition game with the Chicago Bulls so he was not working out. I would talk to Russell first and then catch up with Frazier at his hotel.

I sat in the Garden for three hours that afternoon. Russell went back on the floor and shot baskets for another 10 minutes. He worked hard on jump shots, layups, pivots, taking each shot with moves calculated to fake the pants off an imaginary opponent. After awhile, the players left the floor to change into their uniforms for the photographers. Russell was the last to leave, hanging back to make just one more shot, then another. He sank them with such regularity from every point that it seemed practice was the last thing he needed.

The players returned to the floor in a few minutes wearing their white uniforms. They had toweled off their sweat, and they looked imposing. That condition did not last long, for coach McGuire called a practice. It began with work on a fast break play that swept the floor in seconds. The play was repeated perhaps 20 times with McGuire shouting instructions to players about their positions and movements.

Then the practice began in earnest, with the players

organized in two teams. It looked like a regular game, except there were no referees' whistles, no penalties or foul shots. And no time outs. Again and again the players pounded the length of the floor, on offense, then on defense, shooting, rebounding, fighting for the ball. There was no break in the action as McGuire called for greater speed and increased drive. The players' bodies soon began to glisten with sweat, then run with it. Ultimately it poured in streams from their chins and elbows, as the practice continued unabated for over an hour. The men grew tired and their steps slowed, but under urging from McGuire and team captain Willis Reed, they reached back for new energies and greater stamina. Clearly, the man who could take that practice could play a regulation game without faltering.

The basketball I saw impressed me as a most demanding sport. There was running and dribbling and jumping to be sure, but there was also a great deal of body contact. The players are big men. Most of them weigh over 200 pounds, and they use that weight as a weapon, shoving, pushing, blocking others out of the way. Proper use of an elbow or hip was as important to the play as a fast dribble or a dunk shot. Strength seemed more of an asset than speed.

I watched Russell. On the roster, he was six-feet-five and one-half and weighed 218. He had broad shoulders and heavy thighs. But as big as he was, he was at a disadvantage next to six-eleven Walt Bellamy and six-ten Reed. As he said later, "I'm a little man in this game."

Russell struck me as a guy who came to play. He loved to run and he was fast. Playing forward, he ran the floor, particularly on offense, with abandon, challenging defenders to catch him or stop him. He shot well and passed adeptly. While I couldn't be an expert judge of his basketball ability, I could see that he enjoyed playing. He had a big grin and showed it often. He looked loose and eager and filled with confidence. My impression was that he did not play quite as enthusiastically on defense as offense, but that may have been because of the fatigue all the players felt.

Photographers began to complain about deadlines, so McGuire stopped practice and the men with the cameras took over. The picture-taking and interviewing went on for an hour or more, far too long from my standpoint. Reed, Bellamy, Dick Van Arsdale, Fred Crawford and Howard Komives, the starting team, got most of the attention, but Dick Barnett and Russell, the principal substitutes, got their share. The seven men posed for still and action photos of wide variety. Next, Russell was interviewed on tape by two radio men, including George Plimpton, who has a New York show. Plimpton asked him about Bill Bradley. Russell said Bradley was a great player.

One by one the photographers and reporters left and the players headed for the locker room. Detained by the lengthy radio interview, Russell shot a few baskets, then headed for the locker room. I sat in the arena waiting for him. For company I had two charwomen, a couple of technicians checking out the lights, and Howard Komives. He stayed on the floor for 45 minutes, practicing foul shots and jump shots from the top of the key. He must have shot 500 baskets while I passed the time by retrieving balls for him. During a brief lull, he wiped the sweat from his hands and said, "This is no game for the little man. I got to do something." Komives is six-feet-one and beginning his fourth season in the NBA.

Finally, Komives left and Russell appeared. He wore brown pants and shoes, tan dress shirt open at the throat, a brown and black striped sweater and a jaunty checkered cap. We walked out of the Garden together and got into his car, an elegant dark blue Thunderbird. Clearly he did not suffer from a lack of funds. We drove around the block through heavy Manhattan traffic to stop at a dry cleaners. He darted inside to pick up a suit and some shirts, then drove around the block again to the Paramount Hotel, where the team lived. He carried his clothes and gear upstairs while I waited in the car. This took about 15 minutes. I didn't mind, but the hotel doorman was unhappy to have the entrance blocked by the car, no matter how sporty it looked.

Russell showed up and we drove around the same block again to park in a lot across from the Garden. He wanted to eat, so we walked a half block to a motor hotel restaurant and at four o'clock in the afternoon he had breakfast: three eggs over light, sausage, orange juice, toast and coffee. Breakfast was logical. It was his first meal of the day.

Russell is a good-looking man with a clear, medium-brown complexion, dark eyes, a nose disproportionately small for his face and a large mouth that constantly works into that boyish, face-splitting grin. His voice is smooth and he speaks with great care. Perhaps more than any of the men I talked to, he avoids the mild swear words and improper grammar that edges into most conversation. Later I learned he had minored in speech and radio in college and planned to become a broadcaster when his basketball career ended.

Russell has a catlike quality. He is loose and casual, yet there is tension in him. He seems ready to move into action at any moment. The inner tension shows in his speech. He talks rapidly, with an abundance of words, and conviction flavors every word. It seemed to me that he had thought a great deal about the matters we discussed and wanted me and everyone else to know exactly how he felt. Cazzie Russell was a person of considerable intensity who took himself seriously.

The man who sat there munching toast and poking at his eggs (he ate as though not very hungry) was 23 years old and a product of urban Negro society. He was born in Chicago and reared in a public housing project on the South Side. The project was not a Negro "ghetto," as the word is customarily used, yet it hardly qualified as a privileged neighborhood—or an integrated one. His father worked in a steel mill to support Cazzie, his mother, three sisters and brother.

Russell spoke frankly about his attitude towards the housing project, but I felt there was more bitterness than he allowed himself to express. "I wanted out of the environment," he said. "I read magazines like *Time* and *Life,* and I knew there was another world beyond the one I lived in. I wanted to be part of it. I wanted out of that neighborhood, and I was determined to get out."

The exit for Russell, and he knew it, was through the playing fields. He was a natural athlete and sensationally good. "One of the tough decisions of my life was whether to play baseball or basketball. As a youngster I played a lot of both and loved both. I played baseball all during high school and on semi-pro teams during the summer. I could hit and play either first or the outfield. I used to catch until I grew tall. After high school, the Kansas City Athletics offered me a contract. I certainly was tempted by it.

"At the same time I liked basketball. I was a big kid – five-eleven in the eighth grade and six-three as a sophomore in high school. And I loved to run and shoot. Even as a kid I had a physical need to shoot baskets. The other kids wanted to stand around on street corners. My idea of fun was to shoot baskets. George Washington Carver High School, where I went, had good teams under coach Larry Hawkins. He was a great believer in psyching the other team. For example, during the pregame warm up, we'd deliberately do poorly until the other team finished its warm-up. Then, while the opponents were standing there watching us, Hawkins would give a signal and we'd start dunking the ball. This invariably made the other team nervous and apprehensive. Then, we always tried to do what the other team didn't like to do. If it liked the fast break, we played a slow game. If it liked a poised, play-making type of game, we ran their legs off. He was a great coach and he convinced me to concentrate on basketball. He knew I wanted a college education. He told me I'd never get an athletic scholarship playing baseball and he was right."

As a senior Russell was player of the year in Illinois, and scholarship offers poured in.

"I guess I got 70 or 80 offers and choosing one was difficult. I eventually narrowed the choice to three conferences, the Big Ten, the Big Eight and the Missouri Valley. Of these, I leaned toward the Big Ten. During junior and senior high, I used to watch the Big Ten game of the week on television, and I followed the teams. I guess it was my junior year and I was watching a Michigan game. The team had a 2–12 record. I said to my brother, half in jest, 'If Michigan looks like this next year, I'll go there.' I figured I could make the team.

"There were a lot of considerations in my final decision to go to Michigan. I'd been scouted by Wisconsin, but the scouting report said I was too slow. It so happened that we were playing a deliberately slow game when the scout watched us – so Wisconsin was out. I liked the Michigan campus. Coming from my neighborhood, Ann Arbor seemed like the wide open spaces. And I liked coach Dave Strack. So I went to Michigan."

Russell was as big a star at Michigan as it was possible to be. He averaged over 30 points a game his senior year, became a unanimous All-American selection and player of the year in 1966, and was signed by the Knicks.

In describing his scholastic and collegiate athletic career, Russell made it plain that he was motivated not so much by an ambition to be a sports star as by a desire to escape his environment.

"Even if I hadn't been an athlete, I would still have gotten out of the neighborhood. I'd be in insurance today or some kind of business. I certainly wouldn't be living there."

I encouraged him to talk more about the neighborhood. He did, describing with great intensity the life of a young man who was a loner in a world he considered alien to his nature.

"I always wanted to do something on my own. It made me feel good to take care of myself. I never wanted anyone to tell me to work hard or what to eat or how to keep clean. I could think for myself. I always felt that if I did something just because everybody was doing it that I was getting nowhere. Everybody takes the road to the right and ends up in the ditch. If I take the road to the left, maybe I'll end up in the ditch, too, but at least I didn't follow the others in. I've always thought for myself. If I like what the others are doing, count me in. If I don't like it, I'm not going to do it.

"The thing to do in my neighborhood was to get dressed up, hop in a car and drive around to joints and get drunk. I figured they were driving around and going nowhere. I didn't want any part of it. There was something more out there and I wanted it.

"I wasn't any great scholar, but I maintained a B average in high school largely because I stayed home and studied rather than running the streets. I sang in the church choir and taught a Sunday School class. The people there thought I was great. They would have been disgusted with me if I ran around the streets. Sure, I could have sneaked off, but that would have meant living two lives. I couldn't be that way.

"The kids in the neighborhood labeled me a square. They made fun of me because I didn't drink and smoke and run around nights. When I'd ask young ladies to go out with me, they wouldn't. I was a square. I wouldn't drive around and drink. I'd tell them the guys they went out with didn't know how to drink. All they knew about drinking was getting drunk. I'd tell these girls to think of the future. What would they have? Just a guy who got drunk and beat them up. But they couldn't understand that — then. Now, when I go back to the neighborhood and see some of these women, I know they would like to go out with me. But I'm not about to date them. They are moving all the time, but doing nothing and getting nowhere. I know the people they've gone out with. You put a rotten apple in a basket of ripe apples and you know what happens. These people just aren't in my class."

With frankness, Cazzie Russell had told a variation on an old story, that of the ambitious young man who takes the loner's route to fame and fortune. Does Russell's escape story have anything to do with what happened to him in his first year as a professional basketball player? I think it has a great deal to do with that year, and with his attitude at the start of his second year.

Russell came into the NBA tagged for instant stardom. He was expected to be among the scoring leaders, if not to propel the Knicks to the title. As one of Russell's teammates put it, "Cazzie was built up so much in the press that he was guaranteed to fail. He couldn't possibly do what was expected of him. If he had been an ordinary rookie, everybody would have talked about what a great year he had, instead of what a disappointment he was. The same thing is being done with Bill Bradley. He hasn't a chance of living up to all that is expected of him."

Russell said, "Sure I was disappointed in the first half of the year. I wasn't getting in the game. I was sitting on the bench and who can prove anything on the bench? It got so I could tell how long I'd be in the game, maybe six minutes or 12. You can't prove anything about your ability in six minutes. I just didn't get a chance. If a team is going to pay a man and let him sit on the bench, they either don't think he can play and are sorry they paid him the money, or he doesn't belong in the league. I wasn't playing. I'd be a fool to say I wasn't hurt and disgusted. Everybody said my defense was bad. Was it so bad I didn't deserve a chance? I don't know. I was playing guard at the time. I ran. I passed. I shot. I did the best I could. But so much squabble was made about my defense that you'd think my man was the only one scoring on the other team.

"Everybody was talking about Cazzie Russell. One sportswriter went so far as to call me a pile of waste on the bench. Well, I was too nice to reporters. They'd ask me something and I'd answer. Only they didn't print what I said. If I used bad grammar or talked rough, they'd quote that all right. But when I spoke as I've been taught to, that didn't make good copy. This year I'm going to talk to the press a lot less.

"The second half of the year went better. There were a lot of injuries. When the coach looked back on the bench, there was only Russell. I played more and ended up averaging 21 points a game and making the all-rookie team. I'd hate to think I got my chance only because other guys were hurt. I'd like to think I earned my chance."

Part of Russell's trouble his first year was the early season attempt to play him as a guard. He had always been a forward in college, but the Knicks wanted a guard badly. Russell was fast and he could pass and he could make the long jump shot. If he could make the grade at the new position, he would be that "big guard" the Knicks had long needed. The experiment failed for reasons coach McGuire explained during a brief chat earlier in the afternoon. "Cazzie is fast," he said, "but most of the guards in the league are a step faster. I've moved him back to forward where his speed will be an advantage. He's a step faster than most of the forwards in the league."

The change back to forward accounted in part, I think, for the confidence Russell had at the beginning of his second year. Of greater importance was Russell's mental attitude: he had started to apply in the pro ranks the same approach he had used back in Chicago. He was thinking for himself, being a loner again. He spoke of his plans for the coming season many times and each time the theme was the same: the independence of Cazzie Russell.

"I'll play more relaxed this year. I won't care what people say. I cared a lot last year. Everybody said my defensive game was bad. I got to the point where I'd almost rather sit on the bench than play and be criticized. I sometimes started to wonder if the team wanted me around. This year I feel I can help out. My defense wasn't that bad.

"I can play in the NBA. One year proved that to me. I've shown what I can do. I can run, score, pass. I always was known as a good passer. I'd rather pass off to the open man than shoot myself. I'm good at spotting the open man and getting the ball to him. This year I've got more confidence. I know what I can do and I'm going to relax and do it. I'm going to work on my defense and rebounding. I'm going to do the best I can." He hesitated, as though seeing himself in a game. "And we'll see what happens."

Another time he said: "I know a lot more about the players this year. I know what they can do and what they can't. I know what they like to do and what they avoid. There are guys who don't like to run. Well, I'm going to run their legs off. I like to run. I ran all summer and I showed up in top shape. There are fellows who don't like to move in a certain direction. That's the direction I'm going to make them go. There are players who don't like to pick the ball off the floor. I don't mind. I'll pick up all the garbage that's laying around. I've been working on some new moves. If it was midseason I'd tell you about them, but right now I'd like them to come as a surprise. Eventually everyone will catch on to them, but until they do I might have a little edge."

Again: "I just know my defense wasn't so bad last year. The trouble was that my offense was off. I wasn't scoring. All anybody saw was my defense. You know, when you don't score, you ought to be good at defense or something. This year will be different."

I asked him if opposing players had made it rough for

him because he was a highly touted rookie and had received a big bonus.

"Not at all. They know what kind of a guy you are. You can't come into the NBA and say, 'My name is Cazzie, get over.' I came in, kept quiet and felt my way. Half the season was over before I knew what it meant to be the number one draft pick. I never had a big head. I was no troublemaker. I'm a peaceful guy and everyone knew it."

He stopped for a moment to down some more of his breakfast. But his mind obviously wasn't on his eggs, for he said: "I'm very optimistic this year. I'm going to play my game. I'm going to get myself in better positions. I'm not going to shoot till I'm ready, and I'm not going to pass till the man is open. If the defender gives me some room, I'm going in for the score. I've learned you just don't run over these men in the NBA. You have to figure a way to run around them."

Another pause for a generous bite of toast. "I want New York to win. This is a good team. It hadn't jelled last year. There's more cohesion this year. We're going to be heard from."

A moment later, he said, "I'm proud to be in the NBA. I feel like one of the chosen people. There are only about 150 players in the league and so few ever make it."

Our conversation wandered over a fairly broad area for awhile. He said he was "scared of marriage" because "I don't have anything to offer." He talked about "phonies." He said he could spot them quickly. "The world is full of phonies. There are millions of them. They hang on to you when you're going great, but where are they when you're down? It's hard to find real friends. I've found a few people who like me for the person I am. It's just like being in the construction business. If you're known for erecting good buildings, you'll find good tenants."

But no matter what else we talked about, the conversation eventually returned to basketball. "I'd like to be an established player in the NBA, one who is respected for his offense, defense, passing and sportsmanship. I'm going to forget last year. It will be different this season." I could almost feel his determination.

One game does not make a season, but the next night the Knicks opened their season against San Francisco, winning by two points with a last-second basket by Cazzie Russell. He was high scorer with 23 points.

Talking to Russell, I was constantly reminded of Joe Don Looney. To a lesser degree, Russell had Looney's intensity, his quick mind and wide-ranging opinions. Both men had chafed at not playing. Both were determined to make good in the approaching season. I thought, too, that Russell might have Looney's weakness, his inability to concentrate on the task at hand, his disposition to fret about the coach, stories in the press, attitudes of others. The outstanding attribute of every successful athlete I interviewed, it seemed to me, was the ability to control the mind, to forget the past and zero in on the next play, the next pitch, the next turn at bat, the next golf shot.

When Russell spoke of his determination in the approaching season, he seemed to be upgrading his concentration. He was a man who had come to play basketball, and he wasn't going to let anything get in his way. I wouldn't bet against him. I'd bet he will become the player he wants to be. He's already come a long way as a man who thinks for himself.

WALT FRAZIER

52
JP

Walt Frazier

"Scoring depends upon what you have inside—your guts. If you need the big shot and believe you can make it, you will."

ONE of the interesting things about public figures is that a man's behavior during leisure hours may in no way resemble his behavior while he's on the job. This is commonly seen in politicians and show business personalities, who may turn on a "public face" which is sometimes in sharp contrast to their behavior in private. It seemed to apply equally well to Walt Frazier.

I didn't see Frazier play basketball because of his ankle injury. But I can certainly say that the man I talked to at the Paramount Hotel in New York City didn't seem like a professional athlete. If I'd never met Walt Frazier or never heard of him, and had entered into a conversation with him on a plane or at a party, I would never have guessed his occupation.

For one thing he isn't a giant. The roster lists him

as six-four. Even if that isn't a slight exaggeration, such height is not uncommon. There are men taller than that who've never picked up a basketball. For another thing, Frazier seemed rather slow-moving and unassuming. He spoke slowly, with a pronounced Southern drawl. There was absolutely no cockiness to him. He was shy, quiet, unassuming. A pleasant fellow, but surely he lacked the drive and the ego I'd seen in other athletes.

Yet this impression didn't jibe with his record or with the statements he made. I was continually surprised by the contrast. He spoke of being a team leader, yet nothing about him suggested leadership. One of his skills in a game, he said, was that he was a thinking player who exploited an opponent's weakness. But that didn't come across to me in our conversation. I'm not being critical of Frazier, but simply recording my impressions.

Walt Frazier has an elongated face with a high forehead, eyes set wide apart and a strong chin. A Negro of light brown hue, he had recently begun a mustache, and explained that he grew one periodically, shaving it off when he became tired of it. He wore a handsome tan sweater with a suede finish and expensive-looking gray checked slacks.

Frazier's childhood and his attitude toward it differed markedly from Russell's. Frazier was born and reared in Atlanta, Georgia. His was a segregated neighborhood, but he did not consider it a slum or "ghetto." It was an area of individual homes, he said, and the people who lived there were friendly and neighborly. His father worked in the Ford plant to support his wife, seven daughters and two sons, of whom Walt was the first-born. He spoke of his family and childhood friends with fondness. He credited much of his success to them and said he enjoyed returning to Atlanta to visit them.

"I was always a good athlete, but during most of my childhood I never excelled at sport because I played with older fellows. They were three, four, five years older and I had to struggle to keep up with them. I was never top dog.

"I owe these fellows so much. They taught me to play both football and basketball, not only the rules, but techniques and attitudes. Because they were bigger and stronger, I was forced to concentrate on dribbling and fakes to get around them. They never made it easy for me.

"A group of these older boys sort of big brothered me. When I was young they protected me. Maybe I'd fake out a big opponent and make him look bad. He'd get mad and want to fight. My friends, who were more his size, always prevented that. Then, when I grew older, they protected me from myself. They'd never allow me to drink or smoke, for example. 'You're an athlete,' they'd say. 'You're going to be a pro. You can't drink.'

"Looking back, I realize these fellows taught me to play my best when the pressure was greatest. They used to gamble on shooting baskets. Two groups of fellows would each nominate a shooter and the rest would bet nickels on each basket. I was always the shooter for my bunch. They'd never let me gamble, but they would. Well, the pressure would get pretty heavy. They had confidence in me, and they had what was to them a lot of money riding on me. I learned to do my best in such situations."

Frazier was a high school star in two sports. He attended David T. Howard High, the second largest in Atlanta, and played football and basketball. He made the all-city and all-state teams as a quarterback. "I weighed 185 pounds and I was a good passer. Football was my first love, and I wanted to play pro football the worst way. In fact, I was offered scholarships in both football and basketball. I chose basketball simply because there are no Negro quarterbacks in the pro ranks. I knew that even if the pros signed me, they'd convert me to offensive end or defensive back. I knew I wasn't fast enough to play those positions, so I chose basketball. I guess you'd say I was going to be a quarterback or nothing, so nothing it had to be. When I was growing up, all my friends were sure I'd play football. I guess they were surprised when it turned out to be basketball."

Frazier's credentials in high school basketball equalled those in football — all-city and all-state. He was offered several college basketball scholarships.

"I really wanted to go to a Negro college in the South, one like Tennessee State, because a Negro school was all I knew. But my high school coach said I should do something different. I ought to go to an integrated college up North, he said, where I'd get a better education and have more of a challenge. That's what I did and I've never regretted it. College was hard at first. I had the usual problems of being away from home for the first time, but also, coming from the South, I was behind in my studies. I just didn't know as much as the Northern fellows.

"Southern Illinois was the first school I visited. Later I went to Kansas and Indiana, but I liked the campus, the coaches, the friendly atmosphere at Southern Illinois."

Frazier described his college career with both pride and anguish. "We had a good team my sophomore year and I started on the bench. But after the fourth game, I won a varsity guard position. We had a good year and I was mentioned on some small college All-American teams.

"The next year the team was even better – but I wasn't. I was declared ineligible because of my grades. I sat out the whole year while the team went to the finals of the small college NCAA tournament. That season was the most terrible thing that ever happened to me. I was dejected and utterly disgusted with myself. But I had no one to blame but myself. I'd never bothered to study. I always figured I was in college to play basketball. That year taught me that education was first and basketball second. I knuckled down to my studies and improved my grades one hundred per cent. But that year sure was awful. I died sitting in the stands at the games, and I couldn't go to the NCAA tourney. I couldn't bear it."

His grades up, Frazier returned to the team his junior year, the 1966–67 Cinderella year for Southern Illinois.

"Jack Hartman, our coach, stressed teamwork. What one player did, we all did. I was the star of the team, but if I didn't show up on time for practice or go all out or didn't do the things Hartman asked of me, I was benched. I'll never forget that season. Every time we played one of the big-name, high-ranked colleges we were as keyed up as we could get. They didn't awe us and we knew we could beat them and we did—with teamwork. Maybe they were overconfident when they played us, but we sure did surprise them. And every game was a pressure game, particularly in the NIT tourney at Madison Square Garden. There were big crowds and every mistake counted. We were at our best in those games."

Frazier's words, written down, do not convey his manner of speech, which was so quiet, unassuming, almost diffident that sometimes I couldn't quite believe I had heard him correctly. I found this disparity between his words and his delivery rather disconcerting. There is depth to Walt Frazier and it surprises you, because he doesn't act as though there is.

"Ever since I was a kid, my only ambition was to be a professional athlete. It was about all I ever thought about. But I never had any confidence I could make it. At Southern Illinois, we played against some of the best teams with the most highly regarded players. They were very good, but I realized I could stay in the game with them, and this gave me some confidence. About the middle of last year, some of the guys on the team started to say I'd be drafted by the pros. I sure wanted to be, but I didn't think I would be. The year before, one of our fellows, George McNeil, had been drafted number eight by a pro team. I'd thought how delighted I'd be to be the eighth pick. George hadn't made it in the NBA and that really set me back. I'd thought he was very good. Then there were so many other guys who had had so much written about them but who failed in the pro ranks. I really didn't think I had much of a chance.

"But we had such a good year and did so well in the NIT that I thought I just might be drafted. I still had another year of college, and I hated not to get my degree, but I felt I could always go back and finish in the off-season — if I was drafted. I realized, too, that chances were I'd never top the great season I'd had. Everything had gone just right for the team, but who could say about another year? I might break a leg. Other teams would be primed for us. I figured my value to the pros was at an all-time high. Besides, I was married and we had a baby. I needed the money. If by any remote chance I was drafted, I had decided to turn pro.

"I was as nervous as I could be on the day of the NBA draft. I wanted to be picked, yet I was so sure I wouldn't be. When the Knicks drafted me number one, I was really on top of the world. When they said they really wanted me and offered a generous contract, I couldn't believe it. The Knicks were a young team on their way up. To be part of it, to play in New York, to have the opportunity I have here was the luckiest thing that ever happened to me."

Until he sprained his ankle, Frazier had played in most of the Knicks' exhibition games. I asked him his impressions of the pros.

"These fellows are every bit as good as I expected them to be. I discovered they know what they do best and keep doing it. They specialize. They are efficient. I guess you'd say they concentrate on their assets. Take Hal Greer of the Warriors, for instance. He has certain moves and he gives them to you all the time. He has a great shot from the top of the key, and he's going to keep doing it. My job is to know what he likes to do and prevent him. Right now my problem is that I don't know these guys well enough. They keep using their best stuff on me because I don't know what to expect. Once I become familiar with them, I'll be able to stop them. It's just a matter of time.

"I know I can play in the NBA. Maybe I won't, but I think I've made the team. One man has to be cut soon and another has to go to make way for Bill Bradley after the first of the year, but I don't think I'll be cut. More likely it'll be the big men." Frazier was referring to the fact the Knicks' 15-man roster included five men six-feet-eight or over.

I asked him why he thought he'd make the team.

"I'm banking on my defense. I play good sound defensive ball. I don't expect to score too much, but I'll get by on my defense, passing and play-making."

I was surprised at this. Frazier simply did not project the leadership associated with the play-maker. His manner could in no way be compared to the positiveness and confidence of a John Unitas, for example.

"In the past I've always been the team leader. Once I become adjusted to the pro type game, I think I can do it here. You see, the pros play no set patterns. In college, you are always setting up plays. The leader's role was more prominent. Here, they play so fast and run so much, set plays are less important. Being a good passer is the key. You have to spot the open man and get the ball to him.

"I know I'm only a fair shooter, although I averaged 17 points a game last year. But defense is the key to the pro game. Look at Bill Russell of the Celtics. He's one of the great players the game has ever known, but his reputation rests not on scoring but on rebounding and keeping the other guy from scoring. That's my style. I don't want to shoot much. In the exhibition season I made half my shots, but I didn't take many. This may be a lack of confidence, but I'd rather pass to the guys who can score. Cazzie, for example, is a scoring machine. He's always in the right place. If you get the ball to him, you got two points."

I asked him for some of the specifics of what he'd learned so far.

"The night I hurt my ankle, we were playing the Chicago Bulls and it was a close game. The coach put me in during the last quarter. We got behind and I figured he'd take me out for one of the more experienced men. But he left me in and this gave me confidence. He had faith in me and I got a chance to show what I can do under pressure. I did well, but I hurt my ankle in the last couple seconds of play.

"I just need experience. I got into foul trouble against Greer because I didn't know him well. I know a little better what to expect now, and I'll do better next time. I'll know what he likes to do, and I'll be able to force him to go to his weaknesses.

What weaknesses?

"I don't know yet. I know he doesn't like to go to the inside. I don't know why. Maybe it's a weakness. It'll take a little while to find out. If it is, maybe the way to play him is to force him inside. I don't know – yet."

I asked how he could find out if he only played a few minutes in a game.

"Oh, you can do a lot on the bench. Don't get me wrong. I'm not used to sitting on the bench and I don't like it. But I figure it's up to me to prove what I can do when I get the chance, no matter how brief it is. I sit on the bench and watch the guys. I watch the moves they make and the plays they specialize in. I figure out some things that might beat them. It's like football. There's a coach upstairs observing the opponents and feeding information to the quarterback. I'm doing my own observing. Then, when I get in, I'm ready to go to work.

"This is a thinking man's game. For example, these men are faster than I am. I'm bound to lose a foot race. But I can cope with their speed. I've got to give them just the right amount of room. If I give them too much, they'll shoot over me. If I'm too close, they'll go around me. I've got to use my head and play them just right.

"You have to think in basketball. I've seen all kinds of guys who had great ability, but couldn't think. You have to analyze the other guy and exploit his weaknesses. That's why I look on this ankle injury as some kind of a break. Sure I'd like to be playing, and I hate missing the opening of the season, but I'm getting a great opportunity to study the guys in the league. When my ankle mends, I'll be ready."

But the NBA puts great emphasis on scoring. Would he be able to score enough?

"My scoring will come along. I never worry about it. Scoring depends on what you have inside — your guts. If you need the big shot and believe you can make it, you will. It isn't the amount of practice you get that makes you score. You can make a million foul shots in the empty gym, but what do you do when the stands are full and everybody is roaring? That's when it really counts. I was a pressure player in college. I wasn't the best shooter, but when the team needed the important basket, the team came to me. I could deliver under pressure. When the day comes that I can't handle pressure, I'll quit. I couldn't live with myself if I chickened in a critical situation. I couldn't face myself if I felt I didn't have it inside.

"I don't want to be known as a shooter. I want to be the best all-around player in the league. Maybe I'm wrong. Maybe I should specialize, but I figure I've a better chance by being able to do several things. If my shooting is off one night and all I can do is shoot, then what good am I? I figure that if my shooting is off, I'll get by on my defense, passing, dribbling and play-making. I've already done this. I sat on the bench in the exhibition games and I observed some things. When I got in the game I picked off a few passes. I'd spotted how the guy got open and where they threw to him. I was ready. This surprised them and they respected me. Now that isn't going to work for long. They'll get wise to me and do something else. The point is that by playing defensively I upset the offense. They know I'm going for the ball. They have to watch, not only for the open man, but for me. They have to consider for a fraction of a second what I'm going to do, and in that fraction of a second they miss the open man. I take a lot of pride in defense. A lot of guys don't feel this way. Offense is everything to them. But at Southern Illinois we stressed defense and that's how we beat the big guys. It'll work in the pros."

I was rather stunned by Frazier. He had wisdom he didn't seem to have. In his case, appearances were colossally deceptive.

I had no real knowledge of Walt Frazier's basketball skills. But if mental attitude was the determinant, he would be a great success. He had the desire, the capacity to analyze, the ability to concentrate on the immediate task that I had seen in so many pros.

"You see, I'm lucky," he said as we closed our conversation. "Nobody expects much of me. I can just ease my way in and surprise some people. That's the way I like it."

HARRY HOWELL

A
RANGERS
JP

Harry Howell

"We're playing with artificial feet and arms. Everybody can run, but not everyone can skate, handle a stick and shoot all at the same time."

THE NEW YORK RANGERS practice in a public skating rink in New Hyde Park, Long Island, about an hour and a half from New York City – a low, rambling, white-shingled building whose facilities include public skating, lessons, amateur hockey teams, refreshments and a variety of pinball machines. When I walked in, I spotted a hockey player emerging from the locker room and asked where I could find Howell. "He's on the ice," I was told.

The rink was cold enough to please a penguin. It was so cold, in fact, that the half-hundred or so spectators who'd gathered to watch the mid-morning practice were complaining, and so were the players.

Howell was the only man on the ice. Wearing a bright yellow sweat shirt over his regulation red, white and blue uniform, he was practicing his shots with intensity, banging the puck toward the empty net from 40 to 60 feet out.

I called to him and he came over. Howell is a big man, six-feet-one and 200 pounds. He has a long narrow face topped with wavy dark hair that shows some gray. His eyes are dark and deep-set and his grin is wide and friendly. My first impression was that he was shy and reticent. He said he'd see me after the practice, then went back to his shooting.

I hadn't planned to include a professional hockey player in this book. I knew absolutely nothing about hockey. I had seen perhaps three hockey games, the first more than 20 years ago in Cleveland and two more recently in Baltimore. All were minor league games. I had never seen major league hockey, either in an arena or on television. I knew the object was to score goals, but terms like blue lines, red line, face-off, icing the puck, and high sticking were a mystery to me. Worse, I knew nothing about any of the players. I'd heard of Bobby Hull and Gordie Howe. I could not name a third.

But after I'd done football, baseball, basketball and golf, I thought about hockey and changed my mind. The National Hockey League has expanded. The games are going on national television. Hockey, I decided, had a place in the book.

I called John Halligan, the New York Rangers' publicity director, and arranged to interview Harry Howell, a 15-year veteran with the Rangers who last season had been voted the league's outstanding defenseman. As I set out to see Howell, I was a little nervous. I was wondering how I could conduct an intelligent interview with a player I knew nothing about in a sport I knew nothing about.

I learned a little watching the practice. The other players came on the ice in a few minutes and warmed up with Howell. Emile "The Cat" Francis, the Rangers' coach and general manager, appeared and the practice took on a systematic character. It began with the players skating leisurely around the ice in one direction and then another. Next came a series of short speed-bursts signaled by whistles.

For two hours the team rehearsed various maneuvers. Players went in singly to shoot at the goalie, then in pairs and threes. They practiced offense and defense with two men carrying the puck against one defenseman, then three on two and four on three. The practice concluded with relay races the length of the rink.

Watching it all, I had several impressions. The game seemed like hard work. Racing to top speed from a stopped position appeared to be very demanding on the legs, in fact, on the whole body. I could tell that even these experienced, well-conditioned pros felt the effects of the workout. Yet Howell told me it had been a light one, because the Rangers had a game the next day.

"That relay race is hard," he said, "but we do one in training camp that is much worse. You start at the end of the rink, go to the blue line, stop, return to the starting position, race to the red line and back, then to the far blue line and back and finally to the end of the ice and back. When you finish that one going all out, you've had it."

I was impressed, too, with the amount of body contact

in even this "mild workout." When two players going at full speed crash into each other, it has to sting a little. Then, watching the four on three practice, I had the feeling that play is rather unsystematic. Football and basketball involve contact, but the play seems much more organized than in hockey, which appears to be a mad, aimless scramble.

One other first impression: the uniforms are the most unflattering in sports. The players wear huge, ungainly gloves and thick pads, particularly on the hips, thighs and legs. Over these they don a huge set of loose-fitting bloomers. In many sports – swimming, tennis, track and basketball – the athletes' good physiques are visible. The football uniform consists of enlarged shoulders and very tight pants, so that even a 97-pound weakling resembles an Adonis. But the poor hockey player looks like an Eskimo prepared for a cold night.

The Howell who emerged from the locker room after the practice seemed smaller than the Howell I had watched on the ice. He had after all "lost" two inches of height by taking off his skates and 25 pounds in weight by removing his pads and uniform. Wearing a bright red pullover sweater, he appeared lean, rather than husky. It was difficult to see how he earned the nickname "The Horse." We left the rink and drove to a restaurant some distance away for lunch.

We had a far-ranging discussion of hockey, covering such topics as how the game is played and the men who play it, the difference in attitude toward the sport in Canada and the United States, and the problems of an athlete who sees his career ending. From this conversation, I formed an impression of Howell as a quiet, sincere and modest man who had a great love for hockey and a greater desire to excel at it.

I began by saying I knew nothing about hockey, having seen only three American League games.

"You should see some National League games," he said. "You'd notice a big difference, particularly if you saw them on consecutive nights. National League hockey is much faster and the checking is much closer. Play in the minors is looser, consequently the scores of the games are higher. Where two or three goals will win in our league, seven or eight will be needed in the minors."

I told him that one of the things I couldn't understand about hockey was the penalties. A player would be savagely checked against the boards and it would be perfectly legal. A minute later another body check would send a player to the penalty box.

"Checking is an important part of the game. You see, in hockey, you never play the puck. You play the man. The puck isn't going anywhere by itself. If you watch the puck, the man will skate right around you. An important part of defense is to remove the man from the play by checking and holding him against the boards. This is perfectly legal as long as you use your hips or shoulders to do it. You get a penalty in two ways, either by tripping him with your knee or stick, or for high sticking — that is, raising your stick above his shoulder. Obviously a man can be hurt by either infraction."

At this point, we ordered lunch. When the waiter departed, I mentioned a surprising statistic I had read, that of the 240 players in the National Hockey League only two were Americans. All others were Canadians. I wondered why this was so.

"Given equal opportunity, American players would be just as good as Canadians. In the off-season, I go to a lot of hockey clinics. The American boys of 11 and 12 are as good as the Canadian boys of that age, but when you see the same boys at age 16, there is a world of difference. To be a good hockey player requires a great deal of experience in competition, and the American boys don't get it. There aren't enough rinks, teams or leagues.

"It's different in Canada. Hockey is our national sport. We feel about it as you Americans do about baseball or football. Every Canadian boy wants to be a National Hockey League player. The sports pages are full of news about both amateur and professional hockey, and the players are celebrities. I can remember growing up in Hamilton, Ontario. When "Rocket" Richard came to town it was a big event.

"In the last 10 years or so, football has become popular. Particularly in the Hamilton area, I'd say football is more popular than hockey. But I think Canadians have come to realize that our football is inferior to American football, so its popularity is waning and hockey is coming back stronger.

"Hockey has never caught on in the U.S. The expansion of the league to a nation-wide basis may help, and after the football season, the games will be on television. But hockey doesn't show up well on TV. The action is so fast and covers so much of the ice that cameras have to use distance shots — and the puck is too small to show up.

It looks like a bunch of men skating around aimlessly. I hope television will popularize hockey in this country, but I doubt it."

I asked when he started to play hockey.

"I started playing pickup hockey when I was six or seven. I was playing organized hockey when I was 11. You see, there are several organized amateur leagues in Canada. It's a little different now, but when I was young, you played in bantam leagues until age 14, midget leagues to 16, juvenile to 18 and junior hockey till 20. You moved up in these leagues as your ability warranted. When I was 17, I played junior hockey for the Guelph, Ontario, team. This is on a par, say, with your college football teams. I played with Guelph for a year, then turned pro with the Rangers when I was 19. I never played in the minors.

"Coming up through this system, I played a great deal of hockey. No American boy gets a similar opportunity."

Had he always been a stand-out?

"No, I was one of those fellows who develops late. When I was 15 and 16, there were lots of guys better than me. But they didn't improve and gave up, while I started to come into my own. I was only so-so until my last year of junior hockey. My problem was always that I wasn't a particularly good skater. I had to work hard to improve my skating. In fact, I guess that's why I always played defense. If I had skated better, I might have played forward. As it was, the teams were always short of defensemen. Every kid wanted to be a forward and score. Being a weaker skater, I always played defense. I didn't develop as a skater until I was 16 or so."

What did he mean by being a "good skater"?

"Basically, it's being able to get a fast start. A good skater will be at top speed in two steps. Hockey is a game of starts and stops and quick bursts of speed, so reaching top speed quickly is vital."

I asked about his speed.

"Defensemen are normally a step or two slower than forwards. I can usually hold my own on a straightaway, but if we go around a curve, they lose me."

There was another interruption while the waiter brought our fried shrimp and cole slaw. Then, Howell and I settled down to an uninterrupted talk, which convinced me that hockey differs in significant ways from other sports.

As Howell described it, hockey is a team sport, but a strangely disorganized one. A team consists of six men, two forwards, a center, two defensemen and a goalie. Play consists of two-hundred pound men skating at 25 miles an hour, shepherding a hard rubber puck with a hockey stick, and sometimes propelling it through the air at 150 miles an hour into a small net guarded by a well-padded goalie. There is savage body contact, and on the whole, it is perhaps the fastest, roughest sport played today.

"Hockey is a game of fundamentals that you start to learn as a child. You are supposed to be in a certain spot at a certain time and take a certain action. Winning is a matter of how well you do that. The expansion clubs are surprising everyone this year. They have no big stars, but they are performing as teams and playing good, fundamental hockey."

That statement seemed simple enough. But then Howell seemed to contradict it by explaining that hockey, though a game of fundamentals, has very little strategy and a lot of happenstance.

"We have no particular offensive plays. The object is to bring the puck down the ice and get it to the man ahead of you so that he can take a shot at the goal. We want to take as many shots as possible in hopes some of them will go in. You see, a goal is hardly ever scored cleanly. A shot coming from the outside is deflected into the net off another player's skates, pads or stick. It is important on offense to keep the puck in front of the cage and to keep the stick on the ice so as to get those deflections and goals.

"We do practice defensive plays. We have plays to get the puck out of our own end of the ice and others in case we lose the puck on the opponent's ice. Basically, though, hockey is a game of speed, strength, reflexes and improvisation."

I asked how he could say hockey was a game of fundamentals, if it had little formal strategy.

"I think you'll see it if you look at defense. Hockey is basically a defensive game. The goal tender is only as good as his defensemen, and they are only as good as the front line. If you have teamwork, if the forwards back-check one man beyond the blue line and if the opponents are played one on one, you will prevent a score 19 out of 20 times. The object of defense is to force the offense to the outside and keep the front of the net open. Ideally, a defenseman forces his opponent to the boards. This gives him a bad angle on the shot and makes it easy for the goalie to block it. Most points are scored when there is a crowd in front of the net and the goalie is screened from the shot. He can't block what he didn't see.

"Obviously, you don't always get an ideal situation, but there are still fundamental plays to make. Say you have two men coming down on one defenseman. The goal tender expects me, as the defenseman, to take out the man who doesn't carry the puck. That leaves the goalie with a clear view of the man who has the puck and will take the shot. If the situation is three on two, the object is the same – let the goalie take care of the man who has the puck. This is fundamental hockey. As you can imagine, it doesn't always work. The offense knows what the defense is trying to do and keeps you from doing it.

"The key man in hockey is the goalie. He's the quarterback, the one man who can see what's going on. He's constantly hollering for you to get a certain man or to take out a player you didn't even realize was there. He's the general and we're the troops. Believe me, the goalie has the toughest job in sports. I've seen more goalies who are at their prime walk out of the net and never play again."

I registered surprise at this statement. Howell pointed out the obvious risk the goalie has of sustaining injury from the puck hitting his face or head. "And that's the least of his problems. He's under tremendous mental pressure. If an easy shot gets by him, he feels responsible. He's let down the team. He's constantly worried that the team's otherwise good game will be lost because he let one get by him that he might have stopped."

Howell didn't express the idea explicitly, but he indicated another aspect of the goalie's job which makes it agonizing. He plays a purely defensive position. He normally does absolutely nothing on offense. He can't hit anyone, check anyone. He can't even move very far out of the net. He just stands there and takes it. There is little outlet for his frustration. Other athletes in other sports can "hit back." They get another turn at bat, another tackle, another shot at the basket. At the very least they get the chance to run or jump or do something physical. The goalie engages in limited physical activity. If he is angry and frustrated, he has to suppress it and keep his "cool." If he's under siege at the net, he can't skate up and down the ice to work off his tensions. He has to stay where he is, for he will probably be under attack again in a matter of seconds. He is shot at constantly but can never shoot back. What a mental strain it must be.

The game of hockey Howell described provides plenty of opportunity for outstanding individual performance. Every sport has its superior runner, shooter, or pitcher, but hockey, because it has so little strategy and is played basically man on man, makes the outstanding athlete more noticeable.

"Bobby Hull is the best there is. He can do so many things better than anyone else. He is faster and stronger, and he has the hardest shot in hockey. If he has a weakness, I don't know who's discovered it. I'm in my sixteenth year in the league. I know the capabilities of just about every player in it. Some are strong enough to go through you. Others are fast and will skate around you. Hull does both. If he's coming down the ice toward you, he's strong enough to go through you and fast enough to go around you. You never know how to play him. Most of the time he'll come right at you and force you back, but not all the time. You're doing well if you stop his shot half the time. He's a marvel."

I asked about Gordie Howe of Detroit.

"He's the same combination of speed and strength. In fact, he's just an older edition of Hull."

What about the legendary Henry "The Rocket" Richard of the Montreal Canadiens?

"The Rocket was a gunner. He knew only one thing and that was to put the puck in the net. He didn't like to carry the puck. Back of the blue line he was just another player. But once he got inside the blue line, there was no one like him. He was so fast and had such a great shot, it was heaven help the goalie.

"Hockey has changed a lot since I entered the league. The players are bigger and faster. The whole game is faster. It used to be that if a defenseman was standing up as the puck came over the blue line, he could stop the play. But today you have fellows like Hull. If you're standing still, he'll go around you. Years ago, the Rangers had a player named Camille Henry. He was a power play specialist. He was fast and he had an uncanny ability to get in front of the net and get his stick on the puck for a goal. He'd average 20 goals a year. He was just a little guy, weighing maybe 140 pounds, and he was always being knocked down. But he was so quick he was right back in there with his stick on the puck. But as good as Camille was, I doubt if he'd make the team today. The day of the specialist is gone. We need all-around players, who are good on both offense and defense."

I asked what he meant by specialist.

"There are two kinds. The power play specialist is used when the opponents are a man short. He is usually a fast skater and good shot who may be weak on defense. I was on the power play team last year and that's one reason I scored more goals than ever before. Then there is the penalty killer. When a team is a man short, he goes in to kill the clock. He is usually a strong checker and fast man who can control the puck and use up the clock. But the expansion of the league has done away with the specialists. A team could carry them when the roster consisted of 18 men and two goal tenders. Now it is 16 and two and there isn't room for specialists.

"The style of defensive play is changed, too. I've always been a conservative player. I aim to stay in front of the guy coming down the ice and let him make the first move. When he commits himself, I try to stop him. Defense doesn't have to be played that way. You can go after the man coming down. It's risky, because if you miss him you're out of the play. Years ago lots of defensemen were aggressive, but now nearly all play cautiously. I think it reflects the increased strength and speed of the players."

If the caliber of play has improved so much, how did he account for his longevity? Only three men in the league have played in more games than he.

"I've been lucky. I've escaped eye injury, and I've never broken a leg or had a really serious injury. That may be because I've always had to work hard and I've stayed in better shape. When I was young, I had to work hard to improve my skating. I still do, just to keep up with these faster guys coming along. I've never had a great shot, so I had to work hard to improve mine. I practice my shot as much as I can. A defenseman normally shoots from 40 to 50 feet out, trying to get the puck up to the net for someone to knock in. If you have a good hard shot that goes about a foot off the ice, so it is just over the skates and sticks, then you have a chance for a goal. You have to work at it – at least I do."

How much longer would he play?

"When I started in 1952, I hoped to play 15 years. I did that last year, so now I feel I'm playing from year to year. I'll play as long as I continue to enjoy it and remain effective. I'm hoping to make it 20 years. That's another way hockey has changed, you know. It used to be that when a player was 30, he started thinking of retirement. It was supposed to be a young man's game. But now guys are playing at 35 and even 40. That's good. I always thought a lot of men quit too early. I think they just got tired of playing. You have to love this game. Desire is even more important than speed and strength. When a man has desire, it enhances all his ability. I've always had desire. When I was a kid, all I ever wanted to be was a professional hockey player. Actually I was a pretty good student in school. I guess I could have done a lot of things, but as soon as I was 16 and started to develop as a player, I lost interest in studies. I had to be a hockey player. I couldn't imagine myself as anything else. Even today I can't figure what else I might have done."

Therein lies a problem for Howell – a problem common to many professional athletes. What will he do when he can no longer play? Howell talked about this with considerable frankness. It was obviously something he'd thought about. Hockey has been his whole life, a year-round occupation. During the off-season, he teaches hockey at clinics in the U.S. and Canada. He is 34 now and can look forward, at best, to five or six more seasons. What would he do then?

"I don't know. I have no definite plans. I'd like it to be something related to hockey, coaching perhaps, or teaching. I enjoy working with youngsters."

A career as a coach seems likely for Howell. He has already been designated assistant coach with the Rangers. But if he didn't go into coaching, could he go into business? I pointed out that it was common for well-known athletes to open restaurants, bowling alleys and sporting goods stores or to become a broadcaster.

"Broadcasting is a possibility for me, but going into business poses some problems. I make my home in Hamilton, therefore I don't live where I've played. There is not a single Ranger, present or past, who has stayed in the New York area. There isn't enough opportunity. Hockey players aren't that well-known. No one stops us on the street to ask for autographs. We just aren't big enough names. Now it's different for the Canadians who play in Canada with Montreal and Toronto. They are extremely well-known locally and some of them have gone into business and done well."

I suggested that he must be some kind of a celebrity in Hamilton.

"Oh, I'm better known at home than here. But Hamilton doesn't have a hockey team. It's more of a football town. Opening a rink or hockey school would create difficulties."

Howell was concerned that hockey pros weren't better known in America. "I think hockey will become bigger in America. Until this year major league hockey was played in only four cities in this country, New York, Boston, Chicago and Detroit. Now the league has expanded and the games will be telecast nation-wide. You know, hockey is just about the best spectator sport. People who go to the games love it. There's constant action. In basketball, someone is always blowing the whistle and stopping the action. Football has a lull between every play. Baseball is very slow moving. Hockey is just as rough as football with the advantage of constant action. I think that when Americans are exposed to hockey, they'll come to love it as we do in Canada. When that happens, the salaries will go up, and there'll be more opportunities, in business and in other areas, for players."

I asked how hockey salaries compared to other sports.

"The minimum is $10,000. I'd say the average salary for a player who has been in the league for a few years is about $18,000. The absolute top for a superstar would be no more than $40,000 to $50,000. There's nothing like the $100,000 players you see in baseball, football and basketball. I hope this will change, though."

The waiter came to clear away the dishes and serve some ice cream, then disappeared again. Howell seemed to be enjoying the interview, and responding to his enthusiasm, I asked him many questions, in a rather haphazard way.

I asked him about a man who incurred a lot of penalties. Was he a liability to a team? "That depends," he said. "If a player gets a lot of penalties for hooking and tripping, that's a liability. A certain number of them are inevitable, but if he starts to get one or two every game, he can hurt the team. But if he gets penalized for good hard checking, that can be an advantage. If the opponent knows he is going to get hit real hard when he comes down the ice, he starts to think about that instead of playing hockey."

What was the hardest thing about hockey?

"Getting up for the game. My brother has played both football and hockey. He says that in football the bruises are deeper. You are sorer after a football game, but the football player has a whole week to recover. If he plays on Sunday, he usually doesn't even work out till Tuesday. But we have hockey games three or four times a week. We play 70 games, instead of 14, and the sport is almost as rough. It's hard to put yourself back together physically and to get yourself up mentally. You see, hockey is a game of emotion. There's little strategy and it's man against man, so the players and teams that get up for the game are likely to win. That's the case with the expansion clubs. They really want to beat the established clubs, and they are going all-out when they play us. They're rough. And hockey is a strange game. Unbelievable things happen to turn the game around. Ordinarily, the team that has the advantage on penalties is supposed to score. Maybe once or twice a season, the team with a disadvantage will score. That really kills you. The game might as well end right there. Well, we had it happen in three consecutive games early this year. We lost all three. It's impossible to figure how it could have happened."

Was hockey harder than other sports?

"I think so. After all we're playing with artificial arms and legs — our sticks and skates. Everybody can run, but not everyone can skate, handle a stick and shoot all at the same time."

Does a player have to be smart?

"He can't be dumb. There's no room for the guy who forgets when to check his man or forgets to get in front of the net."

Is concentration vital?

"Of course, but concentration is easier than in other sports. The game is so fast you don't have time to think of anything else."

I liked Harry Howell a lot. He had a quiet dignity, and unaffected honesty. I came away from our conversation with new respect for hockey and the men who play it.

Does the hockey player have the same qualities as the football, baseball, basketball and golf pro? In general, yes. But the sport seems to produce a somewhat different mix. As Howell said, the fast-moving hockey player seems better able to concentrate on the task at hand. He doesn't have time to think about anything else. I was most impressed, really, with the physical demands of the sport. "Everybody can run," Howell said. But a hockey player must be able to skate well, and anyone who remembers putting on ice skates for the first time knows how difficult that is.

Howell's description of the successful hockey player is close to the last word on the subject. "The good hockey player," he said, "must have speed, strength, reflexes, knowledge of fundamentals, but most important, desire. That's what enables you to get your emotion up for the game. And he must have confidence, based on experience. It helps to believe that you are a match for any man."

HERB SCORE

JP

Herb Score

"There are good breaks and bad breaks, fortune and misfortune. But over the season, over many seasons, it is ability, desire, dedication that makes the player. Luck hasn't anything to do with it."

THE CLOCK in the Biltmore Hotel in New York is a famous meeting point, but hardly an imposing timepiece. It is rather small, and it hangs in an alcove leading to one of the Biltmore's restaurants. There are benches in the alcove, and perhaps that accounts for the popularity: you can sit while you wait. The Biltmore is a middle-aged hotel adjacent to the trains and subways of Grand Central Station, and ordinarily it's a busy place, but on this Saturday morning it was quiet. I stood near the clock, waiting for Herb Score to come down from his room.

Many teams stay at the Biltmore, and in honor of the Cleveland Indians, a large orange and black flag hung in the lobby. I wondered what flag would be up next week.

Finally, I saw Score come out of an elevator. He talked

to a companion for a minute or so, and I studied him. He was big, well over six feet tall and weighing about 200 pounds, and tanned and fit-looking enough to be a player. His youthful appearance was fortified by his blond hair, which was crewcut, and, though I'm certain he won't like the description, his baby blue eyes. He was dressed casually in a tweed jacket, sports shirt and loafers.

He came over and we shook hands. He has a broadcaster's voice — deep, resonant, mellow. And he has that quality often present in television or movie personalities — an awareness that people may be looking at him. I felt that he was actually a little shy. He suggested breakfast. I said I'd join him for coffee, and we walked under the Indians' flag and down a flight of marble stairs to the lower lobby coffee shop.

I was going to talk to Score about luck in sports. Sportswriters and sportscasters frequently refer to "luck" or "breaks," both good and bad, which change the complexion of a game. The terms are used to describe a variety of happenstances in sports, including injuries; bloop hits; balls lost in the sun; fans reaching out of the stands to turn triples into ground rule doubles; fumbles; passes that carom off the receiver into the arms of another player; golf shots that bounce off a tree onto the green; golf balls that roll into divots; basketballs that rim the hoop and roll out. Indeed, just about all the "crazy," inconceivable things that happen in sports are ascribed to luck.

Did professional athletes believe in luck? Particularly, what did Herb Score think about it? Today, Score telecasts the Indians' games. In the mid-1950's he was baseball's leading pitcher. As long as baseball is played, the injury he suffered will be spoken of when the subject of luck comes up.

The Biltmore coffee shop is a nondescript place decorated in red and blue. Score ordered scrambled eggs, toast and coffee. As we talked, the place became populated by more than two dozen Cleveland ballplayers, members of the front office and sportswriters. They read the morning papers or talked in low tones while eating. They seemed subdued, which was somewhat understandable since the Indians had dropped a doubleheader to the Yankees the night before, 2–1 and 2–0.

It was 10 years before in a game between these same two teams that Score had been injured at the height of a great career. I've quoted Bob Feller as saying, "I always figured Score would be the one to break my records." Many baseball men held the same opinion: Herb Score was a truly remarkable pitcher.

There are many parallels between Feller's early career and Score's. In his home town of Rosedale, Long Island, New York, Score was a local phenomenon, as Feller had been in Iowa. Score had the same big windup leading to a fast ball that overpowered the hitters. As a high school boy he was a strike-out artist and, in 1952, he was signed for a $60,000 bonus by Cleveland scout Cy Slapnicka, the same man who signed Feller.

In June of 1952, Score reported to the Indians at Municipal Stadium and demonstrated his pitching form for manager Al Lopez, pitching coach Mel Harder, a great Cleveland pitcher of the 1920s, and sportswriters.

He instantly reminded everyone of a left-handed Feller, and writers described the "new Feller" to their readers. Actually, this was an exaggeration. Score threw almost as hard as Feller and he certainly was as wild, but he lacked the brilliant curve Feller had brought to the majors. So Score was sent to Indianapolis, Cleveland's Class AAA farm club, to work on his control and curve.

He did poorly at Indianapolis, winning 2 and losing 5. He struck out 61, but walked 62. He was just too wild. The next season, 1953, he was sent down to Reading, Pennsylvania, a less advanced league. His 7–3 record wasn't much better, nor did his 104 strike-outs against 126 walks indicate much progress. Actually, he was improving and in 1954 when he returned to Indianapolis, he came into his own with a phenomenal 22–5 record. He struck out 330 while walking 140 and was named minor leaguer of the year.

The next spring he reported to the Indians' training camp. Every spring has its clutch of highly-touted rookie pitchers, but many of them bloom in the spring only to wither in the heat of August. The best pitchers typically take a few seasons to hit their stride. Koufax, for example, was a mediocre pitcher until his seventh year with the Dodgers. He didn't win 20 games until his ninth season.

Score was an exception. During spring training, he pitched so many scoreless innings that Cleveland sportswriters began to call him Herb (Thou Shalt Not) Score. He threw as hard or harder than anyone in the majors, and his fast ball was "alive." It hopped as it came to the plate, giving hitters a tantalizing blur to swing at.

I saw Score pitch that first season, on May 1, 1955, when the Boston Red Sox came to Municipal Stadium for a Sunday double-header. There was a big crowd in the stands. The club had advertised it was pitching the "old and the new Feller." What pitching there was that day! Feller, near the end of his career, had another of his great days. Inning after inning he mowed down the Red Sox. In the seventh, catcher Sammy White got a scratch single. That was the only Boston hit. This was the last of Feller's one-hitters, and the crowd roared its admiration for him.

Score took the mound for the second game. Only 20 years old, he was big and strong — and could he ever throw! The crowd "oohed" and "aahed" just watching him warm up, and when the umpire signaled for the game to begin, fans stirred in anticipation. Score wound up and threw. Hardly anyone could follow it to the plate. Strike one. Again Score delivered. Strike two. A half-minute later the third pitch. Strike three. The first batter was out without taking the bat from his shoulder. The second and third batters did better. They swung, but futilely. Score struck out the side on nine pitches. He struck out the side in the second and again in the third. He fanned the first nine batters. (I mentioned this game to Score. He remembered striking out the first six, but doubted he had fanned the first nine men. He had.) The crowd roared with every pitch, for Feller's great record of 18 strike-outs in a nine-inning game was clearly within reach. But in the seventh, Score got no strike-outs and his chance for the record slipped away. He "only" struck out 16.

Score won 16 games that year and led the league with 245 strike-outs. He was rookie of the year. In 1956, he defied the "sophomore jinx" by again leading the league with 263 strike-outs while winning 20 games, five of them shutouts. These two seasons put him in the record books. He still holds the records for most strike-outs by a rookie and most strike-outs by a pitcher in his first two seasons. He was the first pitcher to strike out more than 200 in his first two seasons.

Clearly the Indians owned a pitcher destined for stardom, and he had just reached voting age. Tom Yawkey, the owner of the Red Sox, confirmed the universal opinion of Score's worth by offering one million dollars for him. The Indians, knowing a super pitcher when they had one, declined the offer.

At the start of the 1957 season, Score was acknowledged to be the best left-handed pitcher in baseball. The Indians' great pitching staff had deteriorated and the club lacked punch at the plate, but with Score as the "stopper," the Indians were expected to be in the battle for the pennant. He was good for attendance, besides. Everybody wanted to see the strike-out king, and he seldom disappointed them. And in his own way he was a colorful player. He was not flamboyant, yet he conveyed a clean-cut honesty that appealed to players and fans alike. Before starting a game, or going to the plate, for example, he crossed himself. Asked about it, he explained that he was not praying to win, but asking God that he not hurt anyone or be hurt himself.

Score won two of his first three games, striking out 39 in 36 innings. On May 7, he took the mound against the

Yankees, who had another of their powerhouse teams under Casey Stengel. The Yankees were a big attraction in those days, but the 18,836 fans who came for the midweek game were there to see Score tame the Yankee bats. That would take some taming: the Yankee lineup included Mickey Mantle, Yogi Berra, Hank Bauer, Elston Howard, Gil McDougald, Billy Martin and "Moose" Skowron.

Score finished his warm-up and Hank Bauer stepped into the batter's box. He watched a couple of pitches go by, then swung at a Score fast ball and sent a sharp grounder to third. The ball took a bad hop, but Al Smith, the third baseman, was equal to it and threw out Bauer. One away.

That brought up shortstop Gil McDougald. He was batting .294 and headed for a good season. Score got the signal from catcher Jim Hegan, wound up and pitched. Strike one. The next two pitches were balls. Then McDougald fouled off one. The count was 2–2. It is strange how many baseball fans remember that fact.

Score got a new ball, rubbed it up, then bent over to receive Hegan's sign. A fast ball. He straightened up, reared back into his huge wind-up and threw.

The ball *was* fast, but McDougald was expecting it. He timed his swing and hit the ball solidly. A baseball, coming in at 90 miles an hour, was propelled at far greater speed back toward the mound just as Score was finishing his follow through.

He never saw it. The ball slammed into his left eye and dribbled toward third base. Al Smith picked it up and threw to Wertz at first to get McDougald.

Hardly anyone saw the put-out. On the mound the best left-handed pitcher in baseball had crumpled to the ground, blood pouring from his eye, nose and mouth. Fans, players, coaches and umpires were momentarily transfixed, then a loud groan swept the stands.

Jim Hegan was the first to reach him, then Wertz and Smith. Lopez, the trainer, then all the Indians and most of the Yankees rushed to the mound. They milled around, then backed off to give the trainers room.

Score lay on his left side, arms clutching his face, legs pulled up to his stomach in an involuntary reaction to the pain. Trainers bent over him, but this was no job for them.

"If there is a doctor in the stands will he please report to the playing field." The public address announcer who said it almost sobbed.

Six physicians ran on to the field, including the Indians' club physician, Dr. Don Kelly. They knelt over him and discovered Score was still conscious — in itself a small miracle. A stretcher was run out and Score was placed carefully on it. In the clubhouse he joked, "Now I know how Gene Fullmer felt." Fullmer was a boxer who had been knocked out a couple of nights before. The players smiled, but nobody really felt like joking. Score was carried to an ambulance and rushed to Lakeside Hospital.

Baseball is like show business. The game must go on. Bob Lemon came in from the bullpen, warmed up and went on to pitch Cleveland to a 2–1 victory. But neither team had its heart in the game. Afterwards, the Indians dressing room was as somber as a funeral parlor. The Yankees felt just as badly.

"If he loses his sight, I'm going to quit this game," a distraught McDougald moaned to reporters. He, Bauer and Berra dressed hurriedly and went to the hospital to see Score, but they were turned away. No visitors. They sent flowers instead.

Score's injury drove all other news from the sports headlines all over the country. Pictures of the young star writhing on the ground shocked everyone. Wires, flowers and condolences poured into the hospital from all over the nation. Ernest Robbins of Long Beach, California, offered one of his own eyes to Score "because I love the game."

Medical bulletins from Lakeside Hospital were at best skimpy. Prominent eye specialist Dr. C. W. Thomas examined Score and announced to reporters that the bleeding had stopped. It would be several days, however, before the full extent of the eye injury could be determined. Meanwhile, Score was conscious and resting comfortably. But no visitors.

Score sent out a message, "Please tell Gil I don't blame him for what happened. It's part of the game, that's all."

After a few days Dr. Thomas announced that Score had a broken nose and severe bruises, but it appeared he would not lose the sight in his eye. He would be out of action for several weeks.

The several weeks turned out to be the rest of the season, and the Indians' pennant hopes dwindled to a sixth place finish. Score left the hospital and went to recuperate at an uncle's home in Hagerstown, Maryland. Later in the summer he married his childhood sweetheart, Nancy McNamara.

At the start of the 1958 season, sportswriters speculated on how Score would do. His eye had healed and he had no impairment of vision, but would he be as good a pitcher as he had been before?

Score came to spring training admitting that he felt the effects of the season's layoff, but he set out to get his arm in shape. The Indians watched him carefully and liked what they saw. They could detect no hesitancy on his part. He still took the big stride and drilled in the ball, and after a slow start in training he seemed effective.

With the start of the season, Score's prediction that he would be as good as ever seemed justified. He pitched a strong game early in the season and won. Then he lost. Next he was knocked out of the box. Clearly, something was wrong. Score was not the same pitcher.

What was wrong was a sore arm. Score had felt it right after that first victory, but had ignored it, thinking it would pass. But the more he pitched, the worse it got. Heat treatments didn't help. He went to the doctor, who diagnosed tendonitis and prescribed a rest. Score rested a few weeks, then tried the arm again. The soreness returned.

For the rest of his career Score was just another sore-armed pitcher. He tried, but he was ineffective. He rested and gradually the pain left the arm. But he wasn't the same. The fast ball was neither fast nor alive and hitters fattened their averages on him. He went down to Indianapolis to try to regain his form, but he felt strange on the mound and nothing worked. The Indians gave up on him and traded him to Chicago. He shuttled between there and Indianapolis, then retired at the end of the 1963 season to take the broadcasting job with Cleveland.

When I talked with Score about the injury, he held steadfastly to an opinion shared by many people. He spoke with some irritation. "My injury had nothing to do with my baseball career. That shutout I pitched after I came back proved I was as good as ever. My career went downhill because I developed a sore arm. I was hit in the eye, not the arm." He paused to swallow some coffee. "Pitchers get sore arms every day. It's a risk of the game. I would have gotten a sore arm if I had never been hit in the eye."

Score was sincere, but there are some who disagree with him and believe that the injury unconsciously may have made Score more cautious. Without intending to, he changed his delivery and a sore arm resulted. Feller, who was on the staff with Score, said, "Score's problem was psychological. Warming up on the sidelines, he could throw as hard as ever, but the moment he walked across the baseline to the mound, he was a different pitcher. He couldn't throw hard enough to break a pane of glass. He lost his form, developed a herky-jerky motion and came up with a sore arm."

Score adamantly disagreed with the view that the injury ruined his career. "I just know I wasn't afraid on the mound. Now, if you want to say that starting to pitch after a season's layoff might have damaged my arm, I would say there might be something to that. But I was not afraid. The whole point is that I got a sore arm, not an eye injury. There is nothing wrong with my eye." Indeed, looking into his brilliant blue eyes, one can see no sign of injury.

I had come to listen to Score, not to argue with him, so I was raised another question. Was the injury a matter of luck?

"I can't see any luck in it. If you play baseball, you risk being hurt. A batter takes a cut, misses and wrenches his back. A runner slides into second base and breaks his ankle. A catcher takes a pitch on his meat hand and splits his finger. Injuries are part of the game. If you play, you have to expect to be hurt." He jabbed the air with his fork for emphasis. "Look, I could fall off this chair and get hurt. There's no luck in that."

Was there *any* luck in baseball?

"I don't think so. Sure, players talk about a lucky hit or a bad luck day. Hitters talk about the times they hit the ball well, but right at somebody. At the same time they forget the handle hits they got or the scratch grounders they beat out. Pitchers will lament their good pitches that were hit out of the park, but ignore the bad pitches the batter fouled off.

"I don't believe in luck. The baseball season runs 162 games, from April till October. There are good breaks and bad breaks, fortune and misfortune. But over the season, over many seasons, it is ability, desire, dedication that makes the player. Luck hasn't anything to do with it."

At that moment my interview was interrupted by a tall, lanky fellow with dark wavy hair. Score introduced him as Don Demeter, the veteran Cleveland outfielder, and invited him to sit at our table. Demeter, a soft-spoken man, joined the conversation. Did he believe in luck, Score asked him?

"I went to bat eight times last night," he said, "and I got good wood on the ball five times — but I went 0 for 8. Every time I hit the ball it was right at someone. On the other hand, Joe Pepitone (the Yankee outfielder) was fooled by a pitch and took it on the handle. The ball blooped over shortstop and drove in the winning run.

"All a batter expects is to hit the ball solidly. So I hit it well five times for five big outs. Another guy hits it on the handle and he's the big RBI man. There has to be some luck there."

Score interrupted. "You can't call that luck. It's the nature of the game. It's ability, not luck, that makes a player."

Demeter backed down a little. "There is luck in baseball, but I'll grant you it evens out over a season. Real ability is the difference between ballplayers."

The discussion was joined by a fourth man, Bob Neal, the long-time Cleveland sportscaster. Score told him we were discussing luck in baseball and gave him the benefit of his opinion. Neal shook his glistening bald head in disagreement and, in his mellifluous broadcaster's voice, said, "I'd say luck has a lot to do with baseball. A batter is endeavoring to hit a round ball thrown at maybe 90 miles an hour with a rounded piece of wood. The difference between a home run and an easy grounder is an infinitesimal fraction of an inch on the surface of the bat. Luck just has to be involved. There's luck in everything. Take cards. I know a guy who has the most fantastic luck at poker. If he needs a card to fill an inside straight — there it is, just as if he ordered it. Me? I couldn't win at cards if my life depended on it."

"Okay," said Score, "maybe there is luck in cards, but baseball isn't poker. Baseball is a game of skill, experience and reflexes. It isn't luck that makes a Willie Mays or Mickey Mantle."

Neal wasn't convinced. "Aren't they lucky they never sustained a serious injury that took them out of the game at their prime?"

"That's not luck. Injuries happen, that's all."

"But what do you call it if one guy breaks his leg and another doesn't?"

Score was driven to the argumentative wall and knew it. He smiled and said, "I'd call it misfortune."

I asked if luck and misfortune weren't the same thing. Score's smile broadened but he said nothing.

Neal went on. "Herb, I know you don't agree, but to me you had the worst luck of any player I've ever seen. If McDougald swings the bat a fraction of an inch higher or lower, the ball goes over your head or between your legs. If you throw the ball a quarter of an inch more to the inside or outside, it goes into centerfield. If the swing is a fraction of a second sooner or later, the ball misses you. I'm saying the circumstances were too precise ever to be duplicated. It had to be luck."

Score replied, rather vehemently, "All right, call it luck if you want. But I say I was lucky ever to get into the game. I'm lucky to be alive. I was lucky to find out how many grand people there were who cared what happened to me. I'm not going to sit around and moan about luck. It happened, that's all. I'm lucky it wasn't worse."

He and the others stood up to go. It was time to catch the bus for Yankee Stadium. They said goodbye and walked over to the cashier to pay the check.

I felt Score's attitude toward his injury was admirable. Here was a man who entered baseball with great desire, dedication and talent, became an instant star, and might have been the game's greatest pitcher. He must have been tempted to fall back on self-pity and bitterness, but he never had. I had asked him how he felt when he went back to the minors and worked to get back his form. "I was frustrated and discouraged, and I was worried about how I'd earn a living. Baseball was all I knew, but I was certain I'd find something to do. I never could see any point in carrying on about the injury. It had happened and there was nothing I could do about it but forget it, which I did." Score was applying to his tragedy the mental discipline that seems to be a characteristic of most professional athletes.

I felt that my discussion of luck with Score had been interesting but hardly definitive, and so I asked other pros how they felt about luck. I had been impressed with Neal's analysis of the luck involved in hitting a round ball with a rounded bat. I mentioned it to Feller. In his customary positive manner, he said, "I've known Bob Neal for years. He's a grand guy, but he can't quite accept the fact that ballplayers are paid so much money to play what is essentially a game. I've heard him talk about fractions of inches. He just has to believe players are lucky, not skillful, but it just isn't so. No man builds a career on luck. It's ability that makes one man excel and another mediocre. There are no two ways about it."

A most interesting opinion about luck came from Johnny Unitas, another positive person. "There is no such thing as luck. If you take a break in a game that looks like luck and analyze it deeply enough, you'll see there was no luck involved, only skill. Take an interception. That's a break which may turn a game around. If you analyze the interception, you'll find improper execution. The pass was thrown poorly or the receiver ran the wrong pattern. Maybe the defense forced the interception with a good pass rush or the defensive back correctly read the play and went for the interception. Take a fumble. No luck there. The carrier held the ball wrong or fell improperly. The tackler hit him with clear intent to knock the ball loose."

I asked John about the carom interception. The ball squirts out of the receiver's hands into the arms of a second or third man. "There's no luck involved. The pass play was improperly executed without doubt. Moreover, defensive backs practice catching deflected passes. They know they are going to occur in every game, so they are expecting them, looking for them and ready to gather in any loose ball. Players talk about luck all the time, but I'm convinced that if the situation is analyzed enough, skill or the lack of it will be found to have caused the 'luck.' "

Using Unitas' analytical hindsight, let's consider Score's injury. He was a left-hander with a big motion. He went back on his left foot, thrust his right foot high in the air and propelled himself forward with a gigantic stride that took him far forward on the mound. Many pitchers do this, but Score was unique in one significant respect. A pitcher with ideal form ends up facing the plate, knees bent and in perfect balance so he is ready to cover first base or to move forward or to the right or left to field bunts and grounders. Score did not do this.

"I ended up," he said, "not facing the plate, but far over toward third base. There was always a moment after I released the ball when I couldn't see the plate. I sometimes didn't know whether I had thrown a ball or strike until I looked back to the scoreboard to see what the call had been. If the ball was hit, I frequently did not see where it went until I straightened up and turned around. I remember getting bawled out because I failed to cover first on a grounder to the right side of the infield, one of the fundamental plays in the game. The simple fact was that I didn't see it until too late. I may have been the worst fielding pitcher who ever lived."

In other words, Score had a lopsided delivery that carried him towards third base and left him blind to the plate for a moment or so after releasing the ball.

"Everybody noticed my delivery," Score said. "They pointed out that I was defenseless if a ball was hit back to the mound. Attempts were made to change my delivery, but I couldn't. It was my natural style and the only way I could pitch."

McDougald's smash back to the box hit Score at the instant he was blind to the plate. He never saw the ball.

As Unitas would analyze Score's injury, there was no luck involved. Score was hurt because he had an imperfect delivery which left him unable to protect himself, unable to field his position. The situation which precipitated the injury was certainly not a rare one. Balls are often hit directly back at a pitcher. Sportscaster Joe Garagiola maintains, in fact, that the pitcher has the most dangerous job in sports. He throws a ball which may be hit back at great speed and he is just 60 feet from the batter, which means he has a fraction of a second to protect himself. Garagiola mentioned Score's injury, and Bob Gibson's in 1967, in which the star Cardinal hurler suffered a broken shinbone when he was hit by a batted ball. Another such injury shortened Dizzy Dean's career, after he broke a toe in the same way.

I don't know whether this analysis really proves that luck had nothing to do with Score's injury. I leave the judgment to the reader. The final word may well be that, despite the flaw in Score's delivery, an incredible set of circumstances had to come together for the injury to occur.

Whatever may have caused Score's injury, the pros are reluctant to believe in luck. They are too conscious of techniques, too dedicated to improving their own skills and thwarting an opponent's. They prefer to believe that they are professionals because of their ability, not because they're lucky.

Berry didn't believe in luck at all. The whole concept of luck affronted his belief in the primacy of God's will. Casper, another religious man, also denied the existence of luck, even when confronted with what most men would condemn as bad luck. While I was talking to him,

Casper was called to the telephone. I chatted with his host, who had seen Casper play that morning. Casper had shot a 72, but according to his friend, his score would have been much lower if he had putted better. He had two or three birdie putts rim the hole and hang on the lip. Later, when Casper was stating his belief that skill not luck made a good golfer, I asked him about that day's round. "I would have to say I had poor talent on the greens today," he replied.

Even those athletes willing to admit the existence of luck applied it only marginally to their careers. Cazzie Russell said he didn't believe in luck, but felt "the result of the game is predestined, only we don't know what it is to be." Vince Promuto said he believed in luck. When I pressed him for examples, said, "I was lucky to be traded to the Redskins, where I got a chance to play. I was lucky I ever played sports. If that javelin hadn't gone wild on the playground, my whole life would have been different. That's luck." I asked him if young players need more luck than established ones. "I think so. They need a chance to play and prove what they can do. If they are drafted by a team that has an established player and they sit on the bench, I'd say they were unlucky."

Walter Frazier believes in luck – but only good luck. What most men would consider bad luck, he regards as good. "At the start of my last season at Southern Illinois, I sprained my big toe. That was a big break for me. You see, I'd been ineligible the year before. I was determined to come back big the next year. I worked out all summer. When practice for the season started, I was in shape but

I was all worn out. I wasn't sharp. When I hurt my toe, I had to lay off for awhile. I came back rested and had a great season."

Did he feel the same way about the ankle injury that disabled him at the start of his pro career?

"No, I wasn't tired. I hated to miss the opening of the season. But I feel everything has a purpose. I don't know what good my sprained ankle will do, but I believe everything happens for a reason."

One axiom in sports is that a good team makes its own breaks. What does it mean? I suspect it means three things. First, that a team is so skillful and plays so hard it forces the opponent into errors, the fumble or wayward pass, the hurried throw, the bad pass to an open forward. Second, that some teams and individuals react favorably to pressure, while others do not. Those who make their own breaks apply great pressure to the opponent. This pressure upgrades their own performance while forcing the opponent into errors. Arnold Palmer's famous last round charge for the money is a classic example. Third, confidence forces a result. There is experimental evidence that when a person truly believes something will happen, it does. The person's belief, consciously and unconsciously, leads him to act in such a way that he makes it happen. It is said there are born losers and born winners. I suspect that one difference between them is confidence.

Does luck exist in professional sports? My talks with professional athletes make me think that luck affects performance very little, if at all. I found Unitas' argument rather convincing, and Score's attitude highly admirable.

Breaks, it seems to me, are a product of skill or the lack of it. If any luck exists, it goes to the ablest, most confident players. Certainly no pro builds his career around luck. He'll gladly be lucky, but he'd rather be good.

THE LAST WORD

The Last Word

THE MEN I talked to were all professionals in the athletic world, and to begin with, this was all they had in common. Ultimately, however, it turned out that they shared other attributes.

For one thing, they all loved the sport they played. For many, it was not just a game they enjoyed, but an activity so challenging that it fulfilled them as a person. They had such desire or dedication that they easily, even joyfully, endured the exhausting work and practice which their sport demanded.

All were competitive, but in a way that separated them from many other men. What motivated them was not a hunger for money, power or glory, but a desire, a need, to excel in a tough, demanding activity. The meaning of the word professional is that a man plays for money, but I don't think that is *why* he plays. In every sport, he is competing against the very best. His goal is to excel, to win against that competition, to become a champion among champions.

Far from confirming the popular legend that athletes are "dumb slobs," they were all intelligent men: in the words so many of them chose, they "used their heads." Professional athletics today demands this intelligence from a participant. At the same time, an emotional commitment is also necessary. The competition, the pressure, the man-to-man clash – sometimes involving body contact – of professional sports stimulates an emotional response that "charges up" a player and inspires him to perform at the peak of his strength, speed and stamina. Of course, the athlete who can only achieve an emotional reaction will surely fail. He must think, plan, execute, outwit, outmaneuver. Few activities demand the high level of mental *and* emotional performance that professional athletics does.

The successful pro is what psychologists call "task-oriented." He has the ability to shut out all distractions and concentrate on the immediate task. He does not daydream, woolgather, engage in wishful thinking. He performs. He also has a high level of self-confidence, a quality long associated with the athlete. But what produces self-confidence? I think these men have seen it grow in themselves with self-knowledge and experience. And I think they've achieved this knowledge and experience by exercising a certain kind of courage, the courage to commit themselves to a demanding activity, to risk failure in the hope of success and, sometimes, to endure a great deal of the former before achieving the latter.

So we're back at the beginning, back to two of the questions I hoped this book would answer: are the qualities that characterize the successful professional athlete applicable to other areas, other professions, arts, crafts and disciplines? I think they are. I can't think of an activity in which desire, pride, courage, concentration and competitiveness wouldn't be an advantage.

And finally: do professional athletes deserve our esteem? After meeting the men in this book, I would say that they do. To me, they seemed mature, responsible, self-reliant, confident and dignified. As a sports-lover, I was happy to think it may be true after all that the two words, sportsman and gentleman, go together.

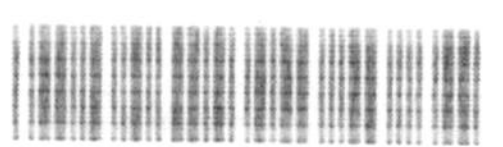